"In the midst of dark times, we need light and clarity. Dan Burke provides both through his illumination of the wisdom of St. Teresa of Avila regarding how we can and must fight the forces that seek to keep us from our high calling to union with God."

—Bishop Athanasius Schneider

"God raised up St. Teresa in the sixteenth century to show the disciples of Christ a way to freedom and maturity in the midst of the tempests of their day. In the twenty-first century, we need St. Teresa's teachings more than ever. How do we battle bravely in our own day? Dan Burke has masterfully, simply, and clearly shown the followers of Christ how to be vigilant against the devil's tactics and take up the torch (and the tools!) to become, once again, the prophets and faithful witnesses of our time."

—Mother Gloria Therese, O.C.D.
Superior General, Carmelite Sisters

"Whatever the reader's stage of spiritual experience, he will surely be enriched by the breadth and the depth of Dan Burke's wisdom in regard to the 'interior castle' and the species of spiritual warfare that transacts specifically in the realm of prayer."

—Timothy Gordon
Author, *The Case for Patriarchy*

The Devil in the Castle

DAN BURKE

The
DEVIL
in the
CASTLE

St. Teresa of Avila, Spiritual Warfare,
and the *Progress of the Soul*

SOPHIA INSTITUTE PRESS
Manchester, New Hampshire

Sophia Institute Press
Box 5284, Manchester, NH 03108
1-800-888-9344

www.SophiaInstitute.com

Sophia Institute Press® is a registered trademark of Sophia Institute.

paperback ISBN 978-1-64413-439-9

ebook ISBN 978-1-64413-440-5

Library of Congress Control Number: 2021949586

2nd printing

This work is dedicated to two women I love:
first, to my wife, Stephanie,
who is a valiant warrior in the Faith,
and, second, to St. Teresa of Avila,
who brought me into the Church
and who continues to hold my imagination
and teach me the Faith delivered once for all to the saints.

Contents

Foreword

by Dr. Anthony Lilles

A difficult challenge and a profound vision in prayer inspired St. Teresa of Avila to write *The Interior Castle*. After years of serving the Lord, founding a new Carmelite community, reforming her old community, and growing in wisdom of heart with some of the greatest saints of her time, St. Teresa wanted to encourage those who joined her efforts to make still greater progress in a life of prayer leading toward union with God. She also wanted to warn them of certain pitfalls along the way. Indeed, in her time, a lack of formation among contemplatives gave rise to serious forms of abuse and caused a real fear of mental prayer in the Church in Spain. As a result, even some of St. Teresa's written works were under investigation and no longer available to those who needed the support of her teachings. Without good theology, contemplative prayer is dangerous, and without contemplative prayer, theology is lifeless. Because of the difficulties and frustrations that poor teaching had caused her personally, St. Teresa realized that the discipline of a prayerful life requires compelling instruction on what it means to progress to full spiritual maturity.

The Devil in the Castle

She wanted to repropose and hand on a safe and expedient path for progress in which her own practical experience of prayer and asceticism was grounded. She knew that such a theological approach to contemplation had to address fierce spiritual battles in prayer against not only the world and the flesh but also the devil.

All Christians, especially contemplative souls, have a special obligation to pursue intimacy with Christ through making personal prayer a part of daily life. Personal or mental prayer is more than the mindless repetition of vocal prayers in fulfillment of some self-imposed external observance. Personal prayer is, above all, the welcoming of the Word of the Father into our hearts and allowing Him to dwell in us in the fullness of His sovereign dignity. This receptivity to ultimate meaning takes attentiveness, time, and silence. The Word Made Flesh will act in our imagination, memory, intellect, and affectivity in accord with the freedom that we grant Him, in accord with our obedience to His will. Because His salvific power always heals and intensifies our humanity, even vocal prayer, to be Christian, must be an exercise of an intelligence of heart bowed in obedient adoration. Such is the personal prayer of the contemplative in the Catholic spiritual tradition.

Today, as was the case in Teresa's day, contemplative souls are meant to be a beacon for the whole Church, a source of warmth and light for all who are seeking the Lord in this dark, cold world. This work is not easy and involves many different hardships and trials, including battles with spiritual forces. Indeed, in prayer these struggles get worse because we "put on the armor of God" to battle "the devil" (see Eph. 6:11). St. Teresa is acutely aware that if those entrusted to her teaching fail to engage this battle in prayer, they could be deprived of a certain encouragement and much-needed source of grace for battles that must be fought in the rest of life.

St. Teresa knew that mature prayer is not a sudden achievement but that it progresses by degrees and stages. Each degree of progress in prayer has special gifts but also specific challenges, including demonic opposition. Teresa struggled with how exactly to convey this wisdom. How could she help contemplatives see at once the greatness to which they were called and warn them of the dire consequences if they delayed in responding to that call? How could she admonish those who desired to live a more prayerful life to resist the inevitable distractions and discouragement they would have to face? It was as she pondered this problem that she received a very powerful grace in prayer, a kind of vision of the soul that would serve as a point of departure and a road map for growth in contemplative prayer. Out of this vision flowed one of the greatest spiritual works on prayer.

Specifically, St. Teresa saw in her heart a beautiful multichambered crystal filled with light. It helped her understand at once the soul in relation to Christ and in relation to the world. She understood it as an image of the soul itself. She noticed that this beautifully faceted reality has many chambers centered around an innermost chamber. The light and warmth flooding the crystal from this deepest source suggest how the truth and love of Christ are meant to flood the soul. The closer one draws to the deepest chamber, where Christ dwells, the brighter the light becomes through the soul's whole crystalline structure. It is also true that the further from this source, the darker and colder the crystal. In other words, the soul is as a living crystal, and its life increases in vibrancy and brilliance the more deeply one journeys into its interior and toward Christ.

Similarly, this image unveiled for Teresa the reality of the soul in relation to the world. The brighter the light of Christ in the soul, the more that soul shows forth into the world as a beautiful jewel that draws others to the Lord. In this way, the soul magnifies the Lord and helps others on their journeys to finding Him. This is the greatness to which God has called every Christian because He has loved us from before the foundation of the world.

Though it is true that not everyone is called to be a cloistered religious and not everyone has the same gift of prayer, all are called to be radiant with the light of Christ. The closer we draw to Him, the brighter we become. He has invited us close. He yearns that we might be where He is, not only in eternity, but even now in time. Christ's desire expresses itself in the universal call to holiness. To say that all are called to holiness signifies the vocation of the whole human family, made in the image and likeness of God. Prayer is how we answer this call.

For every Christian, prayer is meant to be a journey to intimacy with the Lord, a drawing closer to His healing radiance. In this earthly life, contemplative or mental prayer anticipates the heavenly vision that lies ahead. The same face-to-face awaiting us in glory is ours in the shadow of faith when we dare to draw close to the Lord, who has made Himself so close to us. Thus, the pilgrimage of faith in prayer goes from the periphery of our humanity to its deepest center, that place where He awaits us in love. In accord with our love for Him, such prayer must become the priority of our hearts. This is true even if present duties do not allow long periods of time devoted to it. To know this light of His deepening presence fills life with a fullness of meaning and purpose that changes everything, making even what seems most commonplace radiant with God's glory.

St. Teresa also recognized how the image of the soul she received contained a difficult warning. If a soul did not draw near to Christ in prayer, it was vulnerable to the most dehumanizing influences, including the demonic. If the soul was drawn away from Christ and too occupied with passing circumstances, it was possible for the light to grow so dim that the soul no longer provided warmth or light in the world. Without the light of Christ, instead of being a brilliant, crystalline, multichambered castle lighting up God's work of creation, a soul can shrivel in the cold until it becomes utterly lifeless. Instead of being a beacon, the soul can become a source of heartlessness in the world. Yet, made in the image and likeness of God, the human person can never be satisfied or happy with this. We are not created to be heartless. The light that shines in the darkness knows this and has come into the world to deliver us from this plight and to give us His own Heart to be a source of His love and light in a world that desperately needs it.

Demons fear this light and all who would draw close to it because, in the light that shines through God's holy ones, the demons lose their influence over souls and new life flows into the world and wrests power from them. In a world of fantasy, distraction, and anxiety, foul spirits have power to manipulate and oppress. St. Teresa pondered their presence in her vision as poisonous lizards and frogs. Gathered around the castle and even infiltrating its outer chambers, they work to prevent the soul from progressing toward the Lord. At times with great agility and cunning, these adversaries deploy different deadly tactics gauged to thwart the various degrees of spiritual progress in a desperate attempt to keep the soul bound and to erect obstacles on the way to the deeper chambers to prevent the soul from encountering Christ. The more these evil powers prevent a Christian from drawing close to Christ in prayer, the better their chances of snuffing out another source of God's love and truth in the world. Defeated by the Conqueror of death, this kingdom of darkness cannot stand. St. Teresa argues that each soul can choose to make the journey to the castle within and so enter ever more deeply into a relationship with Christ in order to be part of Christ's victory over evil, or the soul can choose to follow the lures of the enemy or give up the journey and abandon itself to eternal peril. What is at stake in this battle is not only the eternal destiny of each soul but all the souls whom each soul influences, including those especially entrusted to it by God, such as family and children.

It makes perfect sense that anyone who would like to progress in prayer will have to contend with these dark forces and, indeed, encounter them with the same steadfast spirit and conviction rooted in the power of Christ that Teresa herself exhibits. This is where Dan Burke's efforts in this present work make such an important contribution. Though there are many commentaries on the degrees of prayer and much spiritual reflection on the special graces that correspond to them, very few souls attend to the spiritual battles to which St. Teresa frequently refers. The tactics of the evil one and how to respond to them are, nonetheless, a constant theme in *The Interior Castle*, and the failure to give this part of the work of this great saint and Doctor of the Church due attention is indeed dangerous, as Mr. Burke strongly admonishes. His methodical presentation of St. Teresa's instruction on the devil's tactics as well as his synthesis of her guidance on how to respond to them make this a very helpful book, one that serves as a worthy introduction to St. Teresa for the reader who has yet to befriend her. It is a battle manual packed with solid counsel and practical application in an accessible, organized framework, and those who desire not to be waylaid by supernatural entities opposed to the soul's union with God will find here an aid for progress into that innermost chamber, where the light of Christ shines forth for the salvation of the world.

The Devil in the Castle

Introduction

⸺◦∞◦⸺

Have you ever considered that the devil is active in your prayer life? In the parish church where you attend Mass? In the lives and actions of people of goodwill all around you? The saints remind us of a key aspect of living the spiritual life that we are wont to forget simply because we can't see it and because we have been conditioned by the media and popular culture to think the devil works visibly only in "bad" people or in extraordinary ways, as in the movies. And although demons are certainly capable of extravagant or extraordinary manifestations, their ordinary work flies under our radar because it just isn't that spectacular, though it is deadly. In fact, subtlety, illusion, and deceit are their preferred methods of attack. An invisible battle for souls is being waged in and around us without reprieve, and we remain ignorant of it to our peril.

St. Teresa of Avila, great mystic and Doctor of the Church, is best known for her writings on the way God leads souls along the path to union with Him through prayer. What many do not know about St. Teresa is that she also observed the actions of demons working with militant force to lead even good souls astray in ways that might surprise you. She shares these experiences freely in her autobiography, which she was commanded to write under obedience to her spiritual director.

In one instance, Teresa describes how she turns cold and tenses as she comes face-to-face with the eyes of two demons during Holy Mass as she knelt to receive Communion. "They are hideous with horns that seemed to encompass the throat of the poor priest," she writes, and she averts her eyes from the demons and instead stares intently at the Eucharist:

> and I beheld my Lord, in that great majesty of which I have spoken, held in the hands of that priest, in the Host he was about to give me. It was plain that those hands were those of a sinner, and I felt that the soul of that priest was in mortal sin. What must it be, O my Lord, to look upon Thy beauty amid shapes so hideous? The two devils were so frightened and cowed in Thy presence, that they seemed as if they would have willingly run away, hadst Thou but given them leave. So troubled was I by the vision, that I knew not how I could go to Communion. I was also in great fear, for I thought, if the vision was from God, that His Majesty would not have allowed me to see the evil state of that soul.[1]

She then reveals the Lord's direction to her:

Our Lord Himself told me to pray for that priest; that He had allowed this in order that I might understand the

---

[1] St. Teresa of Avila, *The Life of St. Teresa of Jesus of the Order of Our Lady of Carmel*, 5th ed., trans. David Lewis, ed. Benedict Zimmerman, O.C.D. (New York: Benziger Brothers, 1916), chap. 38, no. 29, p. 384.

power of the words of consecration, and how God failed not to be present, however wicked the priest might be who uttered them; and that I might see His great goodness in that He left Himself in the very hands of His enemy, for my good and for the good of all. I understood clearly how the priests are under greater obligations to be holy than other persons; and what a horrible thing it is to receive this most Holy Sacrament unworthily, and how great is the devil's dominion over a soul in mortal sin. It did me a great service, and made me fully understand what I owe to God. May He be blessed for evermore![2]

St. Teresa writes of another terrifying encounter with the demonic forces of Hell and the power they hold over a soul who fails to live in a state of grace:

At another time I had a vision of a different kind, which frightened me to the core. I was in a place where a certain person died, who as I understood had led a very bad life, and that for many years. But he had been ill for two years, and in some respects seemed to have reformed. He died without confession.... When the body had been wrapped in the winding-sheet, I saw it laid hold of by a multitude of devils, who seemed to toss it to and fro, and also to treat it with great cruelty. I was terrified at the sight, for they dragged it about with great hooks. But when I saw it carried to the grave with all the respect and ceremoniousness common to all, I began to think of the goodness of God, who would not allow that person to be dishonored, but would have the fact of his being His enemy concealed. I

---

[2]   *Life of St. Teresa*, chap. 38, no. 30, pp. 384–385.

was almost out of my senses at the sight. During the whole of the funeral service, I did not see one of the evil spirits. Afterwards, when the body was about to be laid in the grave, so great a multitude of them was therein waiting to receive it, that I was beside myself at the sight, and it required no slight courage on my part not to betray my distress. I thought of the treatment which that soul would receive, when the devils had such power over the wretched body. Would to God that all who live in mortal sin might see what I then saw — it was a fearful sight; it would go, I believe, a great way towards making them lead better lives.[3]

St. Teresa's writings are replete with references to the devil and his nefarious engagement with those who seek God and those, as revealed in the two accounts above, who don't — or those who seek God but don't understand or engage in spiritual warfare. Her reflections reveal the wisdom she gained through her encounters with the enemy, encounters that also occur in the experience of every soul who seeks to follow God.

Why did God reveal these things to her? The answer is not complicated. St. Paul said, "Be imitators of me as I am of Christ" (1 Cor. 11:1). The saints are given to us by God not only to show us how to become saints but to help us fight the daily battle against the father of lies and his legion of demons. St. Teresa is more commonly known as the Doctor of Prayer; however, those who know her writings well might call her the Doctor of Spiritual Warfare because this is a prominent theme woven through all of her work.

[3] *Life of St. Teresa*, chap. 38, nos. 31–31, pp. 385–386.

Our treatment of her wisdom in this area will focus on her greatest and most mature work, *The Interior Castle*. In this spiritual classic, we have two elements that provide unique insights into the mystic's success in the realm of spiritual warfare: first, her practical wisdom and observations; and second, her understanding of the progressive nature of the life of the soul and how the enemy works to adapt his schemes and temptations depending on where the soul is on the spiritual journey. If we take Teresa as our guide, we will surely gain clarity and wisdom and be far more victorious in our encounters with the forces of darkness as we seek to know and follow Jesus.

St. Teresa deals with myriad challenges and remedies regarding the spiritual progress of souls. Our method of exploration will seek to address only those challenges that she specifically attributes to the enemy of souls and how these can be thwarted or successfully dealt with at each stage of spiritual experience. As with any journey, it is best to plan ahead and know what to expect along the way, from the beginning to the final destination; the journey through the spiritual life on the way to union with God is no different.

You might be tempted to stop reading when the experiences of the journey St. Teresa describes seem so far from your own. This inclination to pause or stop is ill advised and likely from the evil one himself. Why? Because the ultimate tactic of the enemy is to prevent a soul's progress toward God, whenever and however he can. And he is tireless in his efforts. St. Teresa gives a map to the treasure in the heart of the castle, and along the way, she points out clearly where the devil is lying in wait and how he is most likely to reveal himself. The devil's sole aim is to prevent each soul from reaching the goal, and he disguises himself in the process. He will make every effort to waylay you: to get you to pause, to walk another (easier) path, to give up, or to believe that what is good is actually bad, or vice versa. Not only is the enemy seeking to keep you from union with God, but he is also trying to get you off the path and to deceive you and lure you, inch by inch, toward Hell.

You are therefore strongly encouraged to commit to a thorough and reflective reading of this text to become familiar with the wiles of the enemy as he seeks to stifle the growth of every soul. In addition, as you understand, diagnose, experience, and successfully battle against these tactics, you will be able to assist others in growing through the same circumstances and truly live out the spirit of St. Teresa: to support and strengthen your brothers and sisters in Christ in the battle against the devil in the castle.

Finally, a word about our method of reflection on Teresa's wisdom. Because of her wandering writing style, and because the focus of this book is a reflection on her writings, I will quote from her work only when it is directly helpful. Otherwise, in each section, you will be referred to the general location of Teresa's thoughts in *The Interior Castle* itself as an encouragement to undertake a simultaneous and prayerful reading of that extraordinary work, which cannot fail to be of great benefit to you.

The Vision of the Castle

1

The Battles of the First Mansion

St. Teresa wastes no time in fixing her attention on the battle that demons wage against the soul as it seeks God, thereby making the soul aware of the enemy's work to keep it off the narrow way to holiness and union with God. Some castles in Teresa's time had an outer wall protecting the city with a moat, with the city itself inside the walls. Then, deeper in the city stood the castle, with its own walls and extra protection, where royalty would reside protected. Here is an approximate illustration. To keep the illustration focused on our topic, there is no city inside the first wall:

The Devil in the Castle

To better understand Teresa's thinking, imagine that, to be eligible even to enter the castle, some prerequisites must be met. The first is that the soul has been baptized. Think of the Sacrament of Baptism as the first door at the outer gate or as the bridge over the moat (an ancient trench of deep water surrounding and protecting castles). Then the soul receives the Sacrament of Confirmation, which allows entry through the door into the outer court of the castle. This is where the battle begins to pick up in intensity.

Teresa reveals that there are demon "guards" posted in these outer courts — that is, the area just inside the outer gate and outside the entrance into the castle. These dark guards try to keep the soul out of the interior castle. But why? What is the big deal?

The big deal is that there is Someone in the castle whom the demons don't want the soul to truly know. The demons know that, because of Baptism, the soul has a special pass to the Treasure in the very heart of the castle, which is God Himself. By Baptism the soul is an adopted child of God, who desires union with the soul in this life and gives it a foretaste of Heaven, which can be gained only through perseverance in prayer and growth in virtue through a life lived in a state of sanctifying grace, assisted and sustained by the sacraments. But the demons' goal is to keep the soul in a kind of vague, superficial, ineffectual pseudo-relationship to God — one that doesn't compel it to do much more than be nice to others and think well of itself. The demons are very happy with "nice Christians" but not with Christians who are ready to become brave warriors standing against the demons' nefarious cause. When the soul begins to know and truly follow the King of Kings — the One who is in the heart of the Castle — it is healed, strengthened, and released into battle as a warrior in the Church Militant for the Kingdom of God. This is what the demonic guards fear most: that the soul would come to know God and then become a beacon of His light, which pierces and dispels their darkness, showing His people the way into deeper authentic relationship with Him, amassing greater legions of warriors for the Kingdom. The demon guards around the outermost doors to the court want to prevent souls from any access to the One inside the castle.

In her autobiography, St. Teresa reveals the great challenges the soul faces in this first and very ferocious battle with the enemy as the soul sets out on the spiritual journey; but she also emphasizes the helps provided by God to those who sincerely seek Him:

> He showeth great mercy unto him to whom He gives the grace and resolution to strive for this blessing with all his might; for God withholds Himself from no one who perseveres. He will little by little strengthen that soul, so that it may come forth victorious. I say resolution, because of the multitude of those things which Satan puts before it at first; to keep it back from beginning to travel on this road; for he knoweth what harm will befall him thereby—he will lose not only that soul, but many others also. If he who enters on this road does violence to himself, with the help of God, so as to reach the summit of perfection, such a one, I believe, will never go alone to Heaven; he will always take many with him: God gives to him, as to a good captain, those who shall be of his company.

Thus, then, the dangers and difficulties that Satan puts before them are so many that they have need, not of a little, but of a very great, resolution, and great grace from God, to save them from falling away.[4]

---

[4] *Life of St. Teresa*, chap. 11, nos. 6–7, pp. 79–80.

The Devil in the Castle

Teresa also reveals that souls outside the castle come into a familiar relationship with "reptiles and other creatures to be found in the outer court."[5] This relationship is one in which the demon's regular influence causes a kind of familiarity and acceptance of the demon's temptations, though the soul might not be aware of the demonic source. As an example, a demon might regularly suggest that the soul is hungry each time it sits down to pray; or he might offer another distraction when the soul is inclined toward some other healthy spiritual urge, such as refraining from swearing or avoiding the company of people who make one feel degraded after the fun is over. The soul accepts the devil's suggestion as if it is just a feeling that it has, rather than having any inclination that the suggestion is coming from outside itself. This leads to bad habits and to sins that are normative to the soul, and thus the vices and their corresponding demons become "familiar." Teresa says about those outside the castle that they "have almost become like them (the demons); and although they are so richly endowed as to have the power of holding converse with none other than God Himself there is nothing that can be done for them. Unless they strive to realize their miserable condition and to remedy it, they will be turned into pillars of salt for not looking within themselves."[6] They need to look within themselves because demons have no power over us unless we give it to them through our destructive decisions.

This looking within that Teresa speaks of is a reference to the development of an interior life. This is a life of self-awareness

---

5 St. Teresa of Avila, *Interior Castle*, trans. E. Allison Peers, First Mansions, chap. 1, EWTN, https://www.ewtn.com/catholicism/library/interior-castle-12568.

6 *Interior Castle*, First Mansions, chap. 1.

and prayer that allows the soul to become more and more aware of God's will and ways as well as the many habits, rationalizations, and vices the soul throws up to obstruct God's work in the soul and to give in to the influences of the enemy. This habitual examination also brings an awareness of the influences on the soul that come from God (good spirits) and those that come from the enemy (bad spirits). As well, this entire process yields an awareness of self and one's positive and negative tendencies.

The challenges the demonic presents in this phase have many dark facets and, thankfully, a clear remedy. When the soul fails to respond to Jesus' call to deeper intimacy with Him through a life of prayer by pausing or delaying its journey of total self-giving to Him because it is too busy with the things of the world (business, work, hobbies, distractions, and so forth), it can be easily conquered by these demon guards of the outer courts. Jesus teaches this truth in the parable of the sower, in which He describes the enemy stealing the seeds of grace that He desires to give souls (see Matt. 13:1–9, 18–23). Teresa emphasizes how the enemy steals this grace when the soul withholds itself from God and allows itself to be occupied or delayed in responding to Him by prioritizing interests of the world, the flesh, or the devil over its relationship with Him.

Matters of the world are those things pertaining to all the demands of work, politics, finances, and whatever circumstances draw the soul into the day-to-day cares and vices or sins that the enemy desires the soul to be controlled by. As Jesus said, we are to be "in the world but not of it" (see John 17:15–16), but most souls, in the beginning, are both in the world and controlled by the world. The demons desire to keep souls enslaved to concerns about the world and the soul's place in it, instead of concerns over its eternal health and well-being and the need to prepare to undertake the journey to the soul's most important destination: its true home in the Kingdom of Heaven. God desires to set the soul free from bondage to the cares of the world so that it may live in His freedom as His beloved adopted child. When the soul knows this freedom, it can deal with day-to-day challenges without becoming obsessed with or overcome by them and can keep its eyes fixed instead on the One to and with whom it is journeying.

Matters of the flesh are those things pertaining to the faculties and the desires of the soul's lower nature. These are things such as sex, food, fine clothes, material possessions — basically an obsession with anything that feeds lusts or temptations to sensory pleasure. The flesh, empowered by the devil, seeks to enslave the soul to its tastes and proclivities in a way that leads the soul away from God and toward behaviors that are destructive to it and those around it.

Matters of the devil are those related to all of his temptations and designs. Since St. Teresa covers his tactics well, we will leave it to her to reveal fully how he seeks to trap and ensnare the soul through temptation, distraction, and division all along the way into the interior of the castle.

Thus, when seeds of grace fall into a soul that is weighed down by the world, the flesh, and the devil, the soul doesn't see or understand its condition or even the invitation of God because the soul is hardened like the soil and is locked in sin and self-absorption. This is often the cause of anxiety and disease in "nice Christians" who have yet to begin to follow Jesus in a substantive way. These good people often go to Mass regularly, and are generally good people, but are not all in for God.

In the second type of soil, while the soul experiences the mercy of God penetrating its rocky, shallow soil and makes an initial response to the call to follow Jesus, the soul nevertheless cooperates with the demon's proposed distractions, failing to dig deep to cultivate its soil and to allow the healing grace of God to penetrate its interior darkness. This happens when the soul fails to engage meaningfully in the most basic, but most essential, spiritual disciplines, such as regular Sunday Mass, frequent Confession, and daily mental prayer, all of which allow the seeds of grace to take root firmly in Christ. Thus, the soul's roots are shallow, so that when inevitable persecutions or difficulties arise, the grace of God is blown away or withers in the wind for lack of foundation.

The third type of soil illustrates what happens when the Lord's seeds of grace are sown among thorns and the soul allows worries, anxiety, or the pursuit of money, prestige, or power to choke out the love of God; thus, faith fades into the background, drowned out by the noise of life. This noise can be simple distractions that most might count as "normal," such as paying the bills or dealing with a broken water heater. The demons are always delighted to propose a million distractions, a million reasons why the soul can't be successful in the spiritual life, reasons to worry about money, disease, or controlling others or the world around it. All of this worldly worry and noise keeps the soul focused on life outside the inner walls of the castle. Thus, it becomes easy prey for the demons who will pursue the soul with savage intensity at the end of its life. Even if it does not formally leave the Church, if it remains near the exit and on the fringes of the outer courts of the interior castle without ever entering in, the soul is easily picked off at the last moments before death and its final judgment. When the soul reaches the moment of death, it is weak and easily succumbs to the final temptations it faces because it has not used its time and the graces given to it to strengthen itself in the battle of faith and prayer. Thus, at the soul's death, the demons merely propose the same temptations they have used to win the soul over a thousand times, and the soul succumbs again for the last time. It thereby ends its life with a fundamental no in its heart, and the Lord ratifies the soul's rejection of Him and His grace and sends it eternally to its chosen god and his domain, which is the devil and Hell itself.

The fourth type of soil reflects that of an authentic disciple of Jesus. It is deep, rich, receptive, and pure. It didn't start out that way, as no journey begins in perfection, but all the foundational elements of authentic discipleship[7] have been cultivated and enriched and have made the soil receptive for every movement of grace offered by God. This soil is never perfect in this life, but it is ever amended and improved by the soul's willing and daily cooperation with God and His desire to heal it of the wounds, root sins, faults, and other obstacles that impede its journey to Him and so bring the soul to perfect union with Himself. Throughout all of her writings, St. Teresa teaches that this holy receptivity to the will of God comes through worthy participation in and reception of the sacraments of the Church, daily encounters with God and His Word in mental prayer, and a life lived wholly for Him and those whom He has placed in our care.

St. Teresa's final admonition in this first mansion is to caution the soul as it seeks and experiences progress in holiness. As it becomes aware of its sin and need for healing, one of the central temptations of the enemy at this early point in the journey is to turn that awareness and attention to the sins or frailties of others. This causes charity to cool in the soul as it becomes frustrated with the sinfulness it sees in others. At this point, St. Teresa implores the soul to stay focused on its own holiness, daily mental prayer, and deepening Godward self-awareness.

[7] See the discussion on the Paradigm of Ascent in chapter 7.

With respect to staying focused on its own holiness, St. Teresa seeks to have the soul focus on its own sins and need for healing and in availing itself of the means and remedies to overcome them, especially the sacraments and daily mental prayer. Instead of being distracted by the failures of others, the soul should seek to deepen its love of neighbor as it concentrates its energy on growing in holiness. If it can keep itself properly focused on its own journey, it will come to a Godward self-awareness that results in an authentic humility. Humility in this sense is an accurate understanding of who the soul is, who God is, and where the soul is in relationship to God and others. This kind of humility and related self-awareness provide the stepping-stones into the depths of all that God has for the soul in the castle.

Summary of the Battles of the First Mansion

Demonic goal: To keep you out of the interior castle and keep you from understanding what it means to be an authentic disciple of Jesus — specifically, to keep you away from daily mental prayer and a daily examen, or examination of conscience, that would enable you to stay awake and attentive to God's voice and His inner movements in your heart leading you in this new journey.[8]

Key tactics of the enemy
To distract you with:
- Discouragement regarding your ability to follow God or to live the Faith.
- Worries or fear about the things of the world and the flesh: pleasure, money, control, prestige, ambition,

---

[8] See the Daily Examen Guide and the Confession Guide in this book for an in-depth examination of conscience.

work, or anything in life that might be a source of anxiety and that draws you into desolation and away from God.

• Distraction from spiritual disciplines—particularly daily mental prayer and a fervent sacramental life—that encourage deep roots in the Faith and a growing God-ward self-awareness that results in humility. The devil is powerless against a humble soul. To the degree your humility increases, the enemy will have less influence on you.

• Inordinate focus on the sins or foibles of others and a corresponding decrease in your charity for others. A decrease in charity is a decrease in spiritual progress. Focus on others draws your focus away from yourself in relationship with and to God and diminishes charity in your soul. Holy zealousness can easily become angry, bitter zealotry that ultimately paralyzes you by drawing your gaze to focus on the storms, problems, and challenging people around you, rather than on your role in humbly serving God and helping others get to Heaven.

How to battle these tactics successfully

• Begin or maintain weekly, or even more frequent, attendance at Mass. Be sure that you never receive the Eucharist in a state of mortal sin and that, each time you attend Mass, you prepare your heart, mind, and soul in advance to receive the Body and Blood of Jesus in the worthiest manner possible.

• Begin or maintain a habit of Confession at least monthly. Begin the practice of a deep examen on a monthly basis and of confessing even venial sins.

- Begin or recommit to the practice of *daily mental prayer*. A good way to do this is through my book *Into the Deep: Finding Peace through Prayer*.
- Begin or recommit to the practice of a daily examen (see the Daily Examen Guide in this book).
- Be very careful to guard yourself against a critical spirit regarding others. This primary demonic tactic cannot be overemphasized, and a lack of vigilance in this area is a great danger to those seeking further growth. St. Peter's words are worth committing to memory and repeating often, for they provide a tactical reminder of the ever-present reality of the battlefield: "Be sober, be watchful. Your adversary the devil prowls around like a roaring lion, seeking some one to devour" (1 Pet. 5:8). *Don't spend any time focused on the sins of others*; rather, if it is within your control, seek to serve them humbly in holiness. As you recognize their need, seek to serve them in love. If it is not in your ability to influence or to remedy the sin you see in them, then serve the situation through your prayers. Use inevitable piques, irritations, and hurts as a basis for your own examen to unearth your faults and root sins, which you can then bring to God in Confession. Defeat the enemy by using these as opportunities to grow in humility and empathy.
- Consider your final judgment. To be an authentic disciple of Jesus requires you to make a choice to follow Him exclusively. In the words of St. Thérèse of Lisieux, "you cannot be half a saint; you must be a whole saint or no saint at all."[9] Jesus warns us about trying to walk a middle

---

[9] Letter to Abbe Maurice Belliere, June 21, 1897.

line in the spiritual life: "Because you are lukewarm, and neither cold nor hot, I will spew you out of my mouth" (Rev. 3:16). You're either all in or you're not in at all. Period. You must develop a healthy fear of your own sin and of God. You don't fear Him as one who seeks to harm you but as one who can ratify your decision to reject Him and send you to the de facto chosen end of all who reject Him and His provision—Hell.

Spiritual encouragement: As you commit to fight the battle and develop foundational spiritual disciplines, you will get better at fighting. As you draw nearer to the One who conquers all, you grow more aware of yourself, of God, and of the enemy, and thus become less susceptible to attacks and deceptions. St. Teresa encourages perseverance, noting that "the devil is less successful with those who are nearer the King's dwelling-place."[10]

Questions for Reflection

What tactics has the enemy used on
you as you seek to follow God?

What has been the result of the temptations?

What specific actions or spiritual disciplines
can you adopt to fight better against the
work of the enemy in your life?

[10] *Interior Castle*, First Mansions, chap. 2.

Which disciplines do you already have in place that you can develop or strengthen to aid you in drawing nearer to God and so frustrate the enemy's tactics?

2

The Battles of the Second Mansion

Moving into the second dwelling place of the interior castle, St. Teresa reveals that the soul is making spiritual progress, so accordingly it can expect the tactics of the enemy to shift a bit. Her positive indicators of progress allow the soul to assess whether it has reached this realm of the fight yet. She indicates that souls in the second dwelling places:

- practice mental prayer regularly and thereby are progressively drawing nearer to God and virtue
- have an increasing realization of the need to grow in holiness and to keep moving toward God
- have improved in their Godward self-knowledge — that is, have become more aware of their own sin and how they need to reject sin and embrace God's call to holiness

St. Teresa provides an ominous summary of this realm in that she reveals that there is a "fierce war which the devil wages against us."[11] This mansion is more difficult than the last because the soul

---

[11] All of the quotations in this chapter are from *Interior Castle*, Second Mansions, in which there is only one chapter.

is more aware of its sin and the reality of the fight. This means that the soul better understands who it is and who God is and that its sin separates it from God and causes harm to the soul's relationship with God and those it cares for. This can result in several temptations that could sidetrack the soul. One is getting bound by shame. The second is that the soul can fall into self-pity. Both temptations do harm to the vulnerability that the Lord is seeking to work in the soul to revitalize the life-giving reality of what it means to be "naked and unashamed," as Adam and Eve were with God and each other in the Garden.

Teresa also provides a bit of relief as she notes that though the battle heats up here, the soul is in a better place because it has an increased understanding of the path it has chosen and so experiences an increased hope through the sense of progress. This awareness is one that assures the soul that it is doing well as it seeks to orient its heart, mind, body, and life to God. This increased sense of God's encouragement is known as consolation. This consolation is more commonly felt early on, as, like any good parent seeking to encourage a little one as he takes his first steps, the Lord is kind and knows that the soul needs encouragement in these early steps of deepening faith.

Though the soul may experientially perceive more difficulty in this stage, it is actually in a better position and objectively in less peril than in the last mansion because it has a greater understanding of what is happening in and around it. To be sure, less peril doesn't mean there is no danger at all; however, the soul understands that it is moving toward God and away from a life of sin and selfishness that would have resulted in Hell.

The other benefit of this room, and of each subsequent room ever deeper into the castle, is that it is further removed from the demon-infested outer walls and courts of the castle and closer to the center, which is God. As the soul moves in this Godward direction, the enemy has incrementally less power, and as the soul moves closer to the King at the center of the castle, it is incrementally fortified and strengthened. The more the soul draws near to Jesus, the less power and influence the enemy has over it.

On another consoling note, St. Teresa reveals that "This Lord of ours is so anxious that we should desire Him and strive after His companionship that He calls us ceaselessly, time after time, to approach Him; and this voice of His is so sweet that the poor soul is consumed with grief at being unable to do His bidding immediately." This dejection is a kind of sadness that comes from an honest self-awareness that the soul is not fully responding to the love God has for it. The soul aches for God's presence as He draws it in, and it aches more deeply as it grows in awareness of the reality that it is not living up to the beauty and goodness of God's care and concern for it. This ache can turn into something called desolation if it compels the soul to distance itself from God. This temptation is revealed in Peter's response to Jesus when Jesus miraculously fills Peter's nets with fish. In the face of this miracle, Peter realizes he is in the presence of God, and feeling wholly unworthy of His presence and blessing, he suddenly falls to his knees, and says, "Depart from me, for I am a sinful man, O Lord." Jesus' response, "Do not be afraid," was merciful, joyful, and hopeful. He essentially told Peter, "Stand up. You have a job to do. Go and lead others to God" (see Luke 5:8–10).

Even though the fight is difficult, as the soul experiences this beautiful call of God, grace compels it forward. The key here is to be aware of the totality of what is going on and to yield to God's call and the new work He is doing in the soul. If the experience of desolation seems to lead the soul away from God in any way, it simply needs to stand firm in its commitments to prayer and the narrow way and to reject the temptations to focus on whatever leads it away from God and the good.

This increasing awareness of God's voice and work, as well as a deeper awareness of the soul's weaknesses and of some progress forward on the journey, is Godward self-knowledge. This knowledge is different from modern psychological self-awareness in that the backdrop is not a blank slate or some secular ideal but instead is God Himself. As the soul begins to develop an increasingly accurate understanding of who God is, it simultaneously increases in its understanding of who and where it is in relationship to love of God and neighbor. This is the meaning of the phrase "Godward self-knowledge" and accurately captures the perspective of St. Teresa on this matter.

The enemy's tactics in this room may be, or most commonly seem to be, more intense because of the soul's increased awareness, but they don't really deviate from the pattern already seen. His mainstay is to propose and cause the imagination to consider the worldly pleasures of friends, esteem, wealth, hobbies, or occupations of time that don't specifically lead the soul to God and to dissuade the soul from an aggressive pursuit of penance or other vital spiritual disciplines. It is important to note that the enemy will also influence those who have given themselves over to these temptations to get more involved with the soul as an avenue of temptation. Said another way, it is important for the soul to be aware of how the enemy works through others in its life. The closer the soul is to the beginning of its journey, the more power and influence the enemy will have; and in the beginning, it is very common to see the increasing efforts to get the soul to turn back.

Because God is merciful, the voice of the good spirit (perhaps angels or whatever other means God uses to prompt the soul to good) also pulls on the soul and attempts, by reason and the intellect, to help it understand that nothing of this world is worth the loss of its salvation or even its peace. The central battleground here is in the mind. The enemy proposes to the mind the pleasures and interests of life that appeal to the soul's lower nature (sex, wealth, entertainment, or whatever desire keeps the soul from God). The good spirit proposes reasoning against the temporal nature of these pleasures and for the goodness of eternal life in God's company.

What does St. Teresa mean by her use of the terms "poisonous creatures," "reptiles," "vipers," and things like this? These are simply synonyms for demons and the demonic that are found throughout Scripture; such terms indicate the demons' insidious, venomous nature — they are lethal to the life of the soul and should be avoided accordingly. For example, the first universal manifestation of evil most humans experience is hearing the narrative of Satan as a serpent tempting Eve in the Garden of Eden. Similarly, when Jesus sends His disciples out, He tells them, "I have given you authority to tread upon serpents and scorpions" (Luke 10:19), meaning He has given them the power to cast out demons in His name. And there are other references to these creatures as synonymous with evil and the demonic present throughout Scripture.

It is worth reflecting on the way these demonic reptiles and poisonous creatures work themselves into "dwelling places" within the soul. Cracks in character or holes in virtue, sinful behavior, and past wounds and traumas are some of the ways they get in. The more the soul knows of and seeks remedies for its defects and sins, and the more time it spends in prayer, allowing

God's healing presence to penetrate the wounded core of its being, the fewer the cracks and holes there are for the enemy to penetrate into to exert influence.

St. Teresa unveils a troubling truth in this mansion that may be difficult for beginners to understand. This truth is that the Lord will sometimes allow the soul to be bitten or stung by these poisonous creatures. Why would He allow this to happen? There are two reasons. The first is so that the soul will learn to be on guard, to stay awake, and not to fall into complacency or to trust in itself. The devil and his minions never sleep; the soul is fighting an enemy that never ceases to plot against its well-being and happiness in God. God allows or permits encounters with the enemy so that the soul can learn who it is and what it is dealing with, can learn how to call upon Him for help and how to use the helps He has given, and can learn to fight; in this He shows Himself a good Father who cares for His children and wants them to be well prepared for their journey. The second reason God allows the soul to be bitten is to reveal whether the soul is grieved at offending God through its sins and failure to trust in and choose Him over all the false riches and empty pleasures the enemy tempts the soul with. In both cases, it is clear how important these encounters are for deepening Godward self-awareness.

Summary of the Battles of the Second Mansion

Demonic goal: To incite you to turn back to sin and the path to Hell by fighting against your every step toward becoming an authentic disciple of Jesus and thus moving deeper into the castle toward God.

Key tactics of the enemy: These are similar to those in the first mansion, and St. Teresa repeats many of them, so it is wise to reflect on her wisdom—particularly because of her insistence that you understand what is happening. The enemy's goal is to distract you with:

- Discouragement regarding your ability to follow God or live the Faith.
- Worries or fear about the things of the world and the flesh: pleasure, money, control, prestige, ambition, work, or anything in life that might be a source of anxiety and that draws you into desolation and away from God.
- Attempts to weaken your effort in spiritual disciplines that encourage deep roots in the Faith and a growing Godward self-awareness that results in humility. The devil is powerless against a humble soul. To the degree your humility increases, the enemy will have less influence on you.

How to battle these tactics successfully

The central battleground for the soul is in the mind. Thus, to combat the lies the enemy proposes, you must deliberately and frequently reflect on the following:

- The fact that the enemy of your soul desires to get you to turn back and how you must fight against this temptation. A powerful principal you can follow is that, whenever you are tempted, immediately run in the opposite direction. As an example, if you are tempted to lust, immediately reject that temptation by an aggressive movement away from the temptation and toward wholesome activities that will occupy your senses and thus eliminate or lessen the temptation. If you are headed to your daily mental prayer and you experience desolation and a related temptation to deal with some important situation in your life, the proper response is to go to prayer and stay in prayer for no less than the time you had committed to and maybe a bit more. When the enemy sees he cannot distract you from your firm purpose, but that, in fact, you are even more determined to remain steadfast in your commitments, he will generally cease his disturbance.

• The love, provision, and friendship of God that seeks to heal, strengthen, and draw you deeper into union with Himself: the trials in this mansion are an invitation to pray more for strength and to deepen trust in God's loving care of you.

• Your need to begin to orient the entirety of your life to Him.

• The encouraging reality that the more you fight your way toward God, the more the devil will be discouraged and lose his power to lead you astray.

• The reality that you will stumble and fall. You will fail, but St. Teresa notes that "even out of your fall God will bring good." The key is to get up, get to Confession, and keep moving. Never give up.

As well as showing how to focus the mind, St. Teresa reveals other areas where you need to begin to fight:

• You should apply a "great deal of attention" to your spiritual life and begin more purposefully to order to God the time you have at your disposal. For example, the Carmelite sisters for whom *The Interior Castle* was written lived by what is known as a "rule of life" (this is one of the reasons so many of them were so holy). A rule of life is simply a plan for how to daily love God and those He has placed in one's care. You can develop your own rule of life. This can be a simple weekly and daily outline that you review each evening and that includes time dedicated to mental prayer, examination of conscience, and participation in the Sacraments of the Eucharist and Penance.

• You must develop a strong disposition of will against quitting or falling backward. You must fight with all you are to stay on the path that will lead out of this room and into the next so that you can continue to move closer to God in all that you are. For example, saints don't have snooze buttons. Get rid of yours and get up at the same time every day to ensure you give the first moments of the day back to God. Consistent, daily commitments like this will not only help your prayer life but will also strengthen your will against sin and temptation and help you to grow in virtue by creating healthy habits that orient your spiritual compass to the most important realities in your life.

• The Carmelite sisters for whom St. Teresa wrote possessed the benefit of life in community. The convent had a formal system of mutual accountability and support around an organized routine, or rule of life, a core regimen that put their relationship with Jesus in prayer and a sacramental life first. Similarly, if you are serious about growing in the spiritual life, you should have a person, or even a group of persons, who can help hold you accountable to your rule or plan of love, or at least key aspects of it, and support and encourage you in your walk toward the Lord. I am a member of Apostoli Viae, a community of faithful Catholics in the Carmelite tradition. There are many other communities (e.g., Franciscans,

Carmelites, Dominicans, Opus Dei) open to lay Catholics that you can join to help you in this way. The key is to ensure that they are faithful to the Magisterium.

• "Flee from evil companionship." With this advice, St. Teresa offers both a negative and then a positive way to help you stay on the path. The first is to move away aggressively from those who are not on the path to a deeper relationship with Jesus and His Church. St. Teresa doesn't mean to move away from those whom you can and should evangelize. However, if these folks hold you back or successfully encourage you to sin, it is vital that you create a healthy distance and boundaries. On the positive side, St. Teresa advises you to seek out and spend time with those who are not only on the path, but even ahead of you in their spiritual maturity. Spiritual friends or mentors who know where you are headed and have been there themselves can help you navigate the journey and encourage you when you fall.

• Cry out to God. When you struggle, at every point in the battle, you need to be quick and free to cry out to God for strength. Doing this doesn't make the battle cease, but it does put you in right order to your Commander, on whom everything depends. You cannot be successful without His help. When you develop the instinct to cry out to God in your struggles, you will also learn that He is faithful and provides you with the grace and strength to fight and persevere. This is both God's will and God's promise to you, that you learn to be confident in Him, for "he who began a good work in you will bring it to completion" (Phil. 1:6). He always keeps His promises, even when you don't feel, see, or understand how.

• Trust in the mercy of God. It is vital that you recognize that you cannot win this battle or even make small steps of progress without God. You must constantly pray, "Jesus, I trust in You" as you fall and then rise again to fight.

• Practice mental prayer. St. Teresa reminds us that we must draw near to Jesus in order to make spiritual progress and to fight off the attacks of the enemy. She goes so far as to question whether we can even get to Heaven without mental prayer. She further admonishes, "If we never look at Him or think of what we owe Him, and of the death which He suffered for our sakes, I do not see how we can get to know Him or do good works in His service." Thus, without this kind of intimate conversation with God in prayer, your motivation to follow Him will, because of concupiscence and sin, naturally wane. Without prayer, you cannot understand how to follow; without prayer, you will not follow; and thus, at the end of your life, you will end up hearing Jesus say, "Depart from me, I never knew you" (see Matt. 7:23; Luke 13:27). At the end of your life, you will be recognized if you are familiar and intimate with the King of Kings, as one who is not a stranger but a friend. You cannot claim friendship and intimacy with someone you do not know or ever speak to. Prayer is nothing less than an intimate relationship with the loving God who Himself is your life and salvation. God came in the flesh so that you might know Him as both fully human and fully divine. You must commit to knowing Him in the same way you know your closest friend—and more so—and this is done through prayer. Without prayer, you will never find your way into and through the castle. (This book, and St. Teresa herself, assumes you already have a faithful life of mental and vocal prayer and are growing in it. If you are new to prayer, or have not yet committed to a faithful habit of daily mental prayer, please see the "Spiritual Reading and Online Resources" in this book for help getting started in this essential daily practice.)

Spiritual encouragement: As in the first mansion, St. Teresa encourages you with the truth that the closer you are to Jesus, the less real (versus perceived) power the enemy has over you. There are many reasons for this. At the core, it is because the closer you are to Jesus, the further you are from sin. The closer you are to Jesus, the less attached you are to things of this world. The less attached you are, the less power the enemy has to tempt you. St. Teresa also provides ample and powerful advice on how to fight and overcome the temptations and discouragements of the evil one. You will be encouraged as you follow her advice and experience personally what it means to be incrementally delivered from the tentacles of demonic deceit.

Questions for Reflection

Have you felt the call of God to draw deeper
into relationship with Him? How so?

Have you experienced the increased warfare that
occurs when you take a new or more fully engaged
step toward a deeper relationship with Him? How so?

Do you have a written plan of love (rule of life) in place that outlines how you will deliberately give your time weekly and daily to prayer and the sacraments? If not, what is one concrete step you can take in this direction?

Do you have someone in your life you can be accountable to? Are you formally accountable to that person? If not, what practical steps can you take to get this accountability partnership in place?

Do you have relationships you need to "flee" from? If so, what specific steps can you take to create a healthy distance from the person or people who create "near occasions of sin" for you? It would be good to speak to a trusted holy person about this in order to help you devise a good plan and to help you with accountability.

Are you in relationship with anyone who has journeyed deeper into the castle than you? If not, what can you do to begin to find and develop such a relationship?

Do you have a specific time set aside for daily mental prayer? If not, what do you need to do to make progress in this area? Reading and following the program in my book *Into the Deep: Finding Peace through Prayer* can be a very powerful first step.

Are you vigilant in your fight against sin? Are you sorry for the sins you commit? If the answer is no in either case, you know that you should focus more of your energy in each area.

3

The Battles of the Third Mansion

Fear. There is a lot of false teaching about fear in the Church today. Many are turning to a deadly brew of Buddhist teachings blended with Catholicism called "Catholic Mindfulness." Others are turning to the snake oil of transcendental meditation masked with Catholic terminology called "Centering Prayer." Far too many are turning to the deadly Band-Aids of prescription and nonprescription drugs instead of reaching out to God to heal them. The outbreak of a new and fast-spreading illness that arose during the writing of this book has paralyzed even a great many faithful Catholics with fear, with many asserting that it is appropriate to fear disease.

St. Teresa has a different perspective on fear from the one we typically experience. She asserts that it is good to "walk in fear."[12] What is this fear she speaks of, and how can it be good to be afraid? It is certainly not the fear of anything related to the world, the flesh, or the devil. No, it is the reverence of the Lord and the fear of sin. This is not like the fear of a despotic king who cavalierly

---

[12] *Interior Castle*, Third Mansions, chap. 1.

slaughters or harms souls at his pleasure. No, this kind of fear is motivated by love and reverence. It is the kind of fear a man has of his own weaknesses and his corresponding desire to honor his wife whom he loves dearly, and it drives him to distrust himself and place hedges around his marriage. This fear drives him to be a better man because he loves his wife and wants to honor and please her. This kind of fear in love drives out fear of the enemy and the flesh because it recognizes the grandeur and unfathomable power and love of God in contrast to the measly childish tantrums of the enemy of souls. Healthy fear keeps the soul on the narrow way. Disordered fear keeps the soul focused on far less important matters, especially those involving this worldly life and its safety and one's well-being here, rather than the progress of the soul to God and its true home, which is Heaven.

Even a soul as deeply committed to God as St. Teresa is not above lamenting the struggles of this difficult earthly journey. Like a good Jew (Judaism was in her bloodline), she spends a bit of time in her writing arguing with God. In this mansion, she protests the need of the pilgrim soul in the castle to be always on guard against the enemy—never to rest in its vigilance. This helps us to adjust expectations and to understand that the life of a mystic, or even the life of the average but authentic disciple of Jesus, is not one of floating around in ecstasy. The opposite is true. The life of an authentic disciple is a life of both deep peace and joy and epic and exhausting battles. By God's grace, though some battles are lost, the war is always and already won, as long as the soul doesn't give up. The war will be won if the soul abides in Him—if it remains in His love and grace through the means He has provided it with, at so great a cost to Himself.

St. Teresa always points the soul to Heaven as the only place it will find true and lasting rest. Pondering this glorious reality, the soul can know profound peace even as the battle rages within and around it. In the midst of this reflection, St. Teresa returns to the power of holy (rightly ordered) fear and notes that the soul should fear its own tendency toward sin and the consequences of Hell. She notes that many souls have risen to the heights of sanctity and subsequently fallen into mortal sin and have been lost. The fact of the matter is that the soul will fight against sin and pride until the instant it leaves this life. Complacency toward subtle areas of sin—which Teresa will touch on later—and the Pharisaical attitude that can arise when the soul makes a little progress in the spiritual life need to be carefully guarded against because these are exactly the means the enemy will use to trip or bind the soul to impede its progress. Thus, the soul should never assume it will have the time or the ability to repent but instead should remain vigilant all its life. In other words, it must fight like Heaven to get the Hell out of it until it sees our Lord face-to-face.

The following three items are a carryover from the previous mansion but are now a constant in the life of the soul journeying on the castle pilgrimage.

Indicators of progress into the second mansion
• Daily mental prayer is now a habit.
• The soul is clear about the need to grow and keep moving toward God.
• The soul has experienced significant improvement in its Godward self-knowledge.

Following are specific indicators that help the soul to understand and identify whether it has progressed into the third dwelling place. Between the first two mansions and the third, the soul has made notable progress on its journey to God.

Indicators of progress into the third mansion

- The soul has overcome its initial struggles with sin and temptation: this is rightly understood in this context to mean that it has overcome habitual mortal sin.
- It has a strong desire to avoid offending God.
- It works hard to avoid committing even venial sins.
- It loves doing penance—acts of self-denial in reparation for sin.
- It spends significant time in prayer daily.
- It uses its time well.
- It practices works of charity.
- It is very careful in the use of speech.
- It is very careful in matters concerning dress.
- It is very diligent in the management of its household.

A Place to Pause: A Review of the Stages of Spiritual Progress

Because entry into this area of the castle is such a pivotal point in the soul's journey, it is necessary to slow down here and take in the lay of the land. As a map comes in handy for the pilgrim journeying on foot through an unknown land, some discussion of what is happening and what is to come can aid in understanding St. Teresa's perspective on the progress of the soul into the glorious castle of God. It may seem that the notes here are a digression, but they are assuredly not and instead can be seen as essential points of interest and landmarks to be aware of on the entire journey into the heart of the castle.

Following are an updated reflection and a summary diagram of the three phases or ways of spiritual growth (purgative, illuminative, and unitive) from *Navigating the Interior Life: Spiritual Direction and the Journey to God* (for more information, see "Spiritual Reading and Online Resources"). It is intended to be a complement to the commentary on St. Teresa's discussion of this stage of the journey and, if read with attention, will be a great aid to the soul in deepening its understanding of and preparing it for what is to come, especially regarding the ways in which the enemy will shift tactics to create obstacles going forward. The three ways are generally recognized by Doctors of the Church such as St. Thomas Aquinas and St. John of the Cross and are certainly reflected in St. Teresa's mansions. A facility in understanding these stages is helpful as one progresses deeper into the castle. Indeed, one's progress depends on it. St. Teresa often argues that if the soul knows where it is on the journey and what is coming, it will know how to respond to God at each step of the way. Conversely, if the soul is not aware, it will often yield to despair and sometimes abandon the journey altogether.

The diagram begins at the bottom, in the purgative way (the beginning of the journey of authentic discipleship), and ends at the top, in the unitive way (the end of the journey to union with God).

UNITIVE
- VII: Complete Sanctity
- VI: Heroic Perfection

ILLUMINATIVE
- V: Relative Perfection
- IV: Fervor

PURGATIVE
- III: Sustained Piety
- II: Intermittent Piety
- I: Mediocre Piety

The Devil in the Castle

The great spiritual master Dom Chautard, in his extraordinary work *The Soul of the Apostolate*, identifies subphases and indicators of each of the three ways, and I have included these to make this reflection even more immediately practical and useful.

A simple outline of the elements in each phase and subphase relative to the key indicators of spiritual progress follows the diagram. These summaries are approximate and intended to offer the same general benefit as St. Teresa's indicators regarding where a soul is with respect to spiritual progress. They should not be used as absolute, perfect, or even directly linear descriptors of the progress of the soul but should serve instead as a general guide to understanding the progress of the soul.

Phase I: The Purgative Way (Mansions 1–3)

I. Mediocre piety

Mortal sin: Weak resistance. Rarely avoids near occasions of sin but seriously regrets having sinned; makes inadequate confessions.

Venial sin: Considered insignificant and even at times embraced or desired. Hence, the lukewarm state of the will. Does nothing whatever to prevent venial sin or to pay attention enough to avoid it or to uncover and uproot it when it is less conspicuous.

Suffering: Avoids it and experiences complete disruption of peace in time of suffering.

Prayer: From time to time prays well but still in an ad-hoc fashion. Spiritual fervency is inconsistent and fleeting. Prayer is far from habitual but is valued, even if minimally so. Prayer is usually either intermittently attentive vocal prayer or a petition-based prayer focused on temporal needs and desires.

Examen: Not practiced.

Sacraments: Attends Mass regularly and pursues Confession more frequently.

II. Intermittent piety

Mortal sin: Loyal resistance. Habitually avoids the near occasion of sin. Deeply regrets sin when recognized. Does penance to make reparation. Makes adequate confessions with some contrition and purpose of amendment.

Venial sin: Sometimes deliberate. Puts up a weak fight. Sorrow is only superficial. Makes an examination of conscience but without any method, preparation, or tangible plan of mitigation.

Suffering: Tolerates it with complaining but with little peace.

Prayer: Practices vocal prayer regularly. Not yet firmly resolved to remain faithful to structured meditation (time, place, topic, and material). Often gives up as soon as dryness is felt or as soon as there is business to attend to.

Examen: Practiced intermittently.

Sacraments: Attends Mass weekly and pursues Confession at least quarterly.

III. Sustained piety

Mortal sin: Very rare and only when taken suddenly by surprise, and then often it is to be doubted if the sin is mortal. It is followed by ardent feelings of guilt and a desire for penance.

Venial sin: Not habitual. Vigilant in avoiding and fighting it and rarely deliberate. Intense sorrow, but does little by way of reparation. Consistent particular examen but aiming only at avoidance of venial sin. Makes good confessions with a firm purpose of amendment. Takes venial sins to Confession.

Imperfections: Either avoids uncovering them so as not to have to fight them or else easily excuses them. Approves the thought of renouncing them, and would like to do so, but makes little effort in that direction.

Suffering: Embraces it and endures it with relative peace but still struggles.

Prayer: Consistently faithful to specific time and approach to prayer, no matter what happens. This prayer includes vocal prayer and meditation that is often affective. Prayer of simplicity may emerge. Alternating consolations and dryness, the latter endured with considerable hardship. Contemplative aridity often surfaces here or in the Fervor stage.

Examen: Practiced at least once daily—often more than once.

Sacraments: Always attends weekly and daily Mass if able. Pursues Confession on a regular schedule.

Phase II: The Illuminitive Way (Mansions 4–6)

IV. Fervor

Venial sin: Never deliberate. By surprise, sometimes, or with imperfect advertence. Keenly regretted and serious reparation made.

Imperfections: Wants nothing to do with them. Watches over them, fights them with courage and diligence in order to be more pleasing to God. Still, imperfections are sometimes accepted, though regretted at once. Frequent acts of renunciation. Particular examen aims at perfection in a specific virtue.

Prayer: Vocal and mental prayer is constantly practiced and gladly prolonged. Prayer is often affective, and the prayer of simplicity or of quiet. Alternation between powerful consolations and fierce trials.

Examen: Practiced at least twice daily.

Suffering: Embraced with clear understanding of the benefit, some joy, and peace.

Sacraments: Fervently participates in weekly and daily Mass if able. Pursues Confession at least on a monthly basis. Imperfections are offered in Confession for the purpose of obtaining the grace necessary to overcome them (i.e., devotional Confession).

V. Relative perfection

Imperfections: Guards against them energetically and with much care and love. They happen only with half advertence.

Suffering: Joyfully embraced with peace and sometimes pursued for the sake of others.

Prayer: Habitual life of prayer, even when occupied in external works. Thirst for self-renunciation, annihilation, detachment, and divine love. Hunger for the Eucharist and for Heaven. Graces of infused prayer, of different degrees. Often passive purification.

Phase III: The Unitive Way (Mansions 6–7)

VI. Heroic perfection

Imperfections: Nothing but the first impulse.

Suffering: Joyfully embraced and pursued for the sake of others.

Prayer: Supernatural graces of contemplation sometimes accompanied by extraordinary phenomena. Pronounced passive purifications. Contempt of self to the point of complete self-forgetfulness. Prefers suffering to joys.

VII. Complete sanctity

Imperfections: Hardly apparent and rare.

Prayer: Frequently experience the transforming union. Spiritual marriage. Purifications by love. Ardent thirst for sufferings and humiliations for the sake of others.

This summary provides a basic understanding of where the soul began and where it has progressed upon entering the third mansion. To align the mansions with the three ways, the third mansion corresponds to end of the late purgative way or an over-lap between the late purgative and early illuminative way.

This framework for understanding spiritual progress can fill in many practical gaps for the soul desiring to understand and make firm commitments to yield to and cooperate with God's grace and to see progress over time. Many of these elements are mentioned in the writings of St. Teresa and St. John of the Cross. Others are assumed or taken for granted as present in various stages because they are normative for the life of a disciple of Jesus. Reflection on this framework, at least annually, is a powerful aid in setting the course for each year as the soul fights to move closer and closer to the center of the castle, where the King of Kings dwells and where the spiritual battle with the enemy is far less challenging or intimidating.

One unique characteristic of the third mansion is that it is a transitional space from the purgative to the illuminative way and so presents unique battles on the journey. St. Teresa reveals one particular struggle, that of aridity, that arises in the late purgative stage and beyond. Aridity is often experienced as the absence of any sense of the presence of God. Prayer becomes dry, and perhaps it is more difficult for the soul to "show up" for time with God. The soul does desire to pray, but the difficulty lies in the new experience of prayer, which can be frustrating. Distractions may resurface, spiritual things may lose a bit of their luster, and the soul can be tempted to cut corners, cut time short, or ease up because it is not "getting anything" out of its time of prayer on an emotional or sensory level in the way it did when it first began. This "feeling state" is a key battleground and must be prepared for with diligence.

The central cause of aridity in this phase is that the soul is still attached to created things and feelings. Recall the rich young man who walked away from Jesus, and probably ultimately into Hell, because he was so attached to his wealth that he could not choose Christ and Heaven over his worldly riches (see Matt. 19:16–22). Similarly, the soul feels some aversion to continuing on with the spiritual life because it doesn't feel as good as it did early on and it is becoming clear to it that certain sacrifices of even objectively good things need to be made. One might compare this stage to the post-honeymoon phase of a marriage, when sensations have cooled and the day-to-day routine sets in and the intensity and pleasure of the early days presents itself only occasionally. The rich young man had made much progress: when he met Jesus, he had a good list of spiritual fruit. However, when Jesus invited him to give up the one thing that blocked his progress, he declined and walked away from his Savior and, presumably, his salvation.

Similarly, when a soul comes to the end of the purgative way, tough but crucial decisions must be made. Having gained greater self-knowledge through hard-won spiritual battles with the enemy and its own sin and brokenness, the soul is empowered with greater clarity about what hinders it. The soul now comes to another place in which it engages the thousands of decision points regarding confirming its choice of path in life: Will it follow the world, the flesh, and the devil, or will it continue diligently to follow God and to remain what it has already progressed, by God's grace, to become—an authentic disciple? It may seem like a trivial matter, but many saints and Doctors of the Church, including St. Teresa, have lamented over the number of souls lost in this transitional period of the journey. These souls, by the grace of God and their own cooperation, have fought off all their mortal sins, and maybe even venial sins, but fail to keep on fighting to abide in God through the active rejection and renunciation of trivial attachments that keep them tethered to the path to Hell.

Of some encouragement is the fact that, as the soul begins to emerge out of the purgative way, it is confronted with these attachments when it is, by long conditioning in ascesis (self-giving and self-denial), relatively strong in will. The soul's will is stronger by the time it reaches this point because it has practiced spiritual disciplines for years All of the spiritual exercises that are now firm habits have given it the ability to fight well. However, it still faces difficult choices, depending on its attachments, and often these are subtle and may even be attachments to apparent goods that the enemy will deceive the soul into rationalizing and excusing away as harmless, as long as the soul is distracted or lured away from attaching to God alone, who is the only Good. Like the rich young man, who had made much progress by the time he met Jesus, so, too, many pilgrims in the castle progress steadily to the point of this meeting. They are not yet in the center of the castle, but Jesus continually, at key moments, comes to invite them to leave behind whatever hinders them so that they can enter more deeply into the castle, into Him and life in Him alone. Only those who respond positively and agree to let go of all of their worldly impediments, whatever they may be, continue in their progress. Those who don't let go enter a lukewarm state and, soon after, begin to regress.

The way to the center of the castle is through the shedding of all loves, interests, aspirations, and cares that are not of God or that fail to lead the soul to God—even those that might be considered "good" in and of themselves, and this is the difficulty for many souls in this place.

The entire battle up to this point has yielded one of the most important virtues in a soul that ultimately finds its way to the center of the castle: humility. Within this deeper humility, the soul is clearer about who and what it is and who God is. The soul more clearly understands the mercy of God in its redemption. The soul now knows how to yield to God better and more instinctively and thus is able to submit to a new and very difficult challenge in its prayer life: contemplative aridity, a gift designed to lead the soul into deeper union. This is not aridity or desolation that comes from having neglected spiritual disciplines, or from failing to manage health or sleep, or from the Lord's allowing a challenge to strengthen the soul. Instead, this is a kind of aridity that, accompanied by a few key signs, reveals that the Lord is doing a deeper work to bring the soul closer to Himself. These signs are straightforward and revealed by both St. John of the Cross and St. Teresa of Avila:

- *Vice and virtue:* Mortal sin—not present; venial sin— fading and not habitual; virtue—developing.
- *Detachment:* Detached from worldly things with a sufficient measure of strength and the ability to endure dryness in prayer, even for sustained periods. Distaste for vain conversation and other forms of worldly engagement.
- *Spiritual disciplines:* Exercised for a time in the way of virtue and perseverance in mental prayer.
- *Aridity or dryness:* Neither pleasure nor consolation in the things of God or in material or created things; or a certain kind of desolation.
- *Desire:* Strongly drawn to be alone with God in spite of aridity.
- *Prayer:* Lack of desire and inability to practice discursive meditation or receive satisfaction from it as before; the lack of desire to use the imagination in prayer in any form. Not necessarily free from distractions or a

wandering imagination. Even so, the soul does experience an ability to exercise a general, loving focus on God.

Contemplative aridity is not caused by spiritual sloth or any of the heretofore normal frailties of the immature soul. As it seeks to enter into prayer, the soul desires to be there in prayer and with God, but it struggles to understand what is happening to it, since its experience of prayer is now so changed and the soul is unable to pray as it has so fruitfully in the past. When, in this stage of growth, the soul experiences this aridity, the devil seeks to make it restless and discouraged, so that it will seek out things other than the discomfort of its spiritual exercises and so draw it away from committed time and attention to God. St. Teresa proposes that, rather than give in to this discouragement and seek to assuage the strangeness of it, the soul should seek to acquire an even deeper humility.

The soul cannot, in a direct way, overcome this aridity by any agency of the will. It must do what it can to persevere and keep showing up for prayer. This is the soul's part in the battle—just to keep showing up—and it is a very important challenge: the soul may think its efforts are all for nothing, but it is crucial for the soul to remain steadfast and hold to its practice of prayer, regardless of how it feels. The rest is up to God. The soul must endure the trial of aridity and trust God to bring it out of this desert if and when He determines to do so. The soul must remain in Him, and this remaining is a waiting in the desert that is sustained by trust in God and His presence, even though it cannot be felt, and the humble hope that He will heal and draw the soul forth when He knows it is ready for the next phase of the journey to enter more deeply into His heart.

St. Teresa emphasizes the need to rest content and at peace with this aridity, to yield to this challenging work of God, even if it remains for extended periods. The ebb and flow of the severity of contemplative aridity is common, but in some souls, God desires a deeper work of purification that can come only through a prolonged process of stripping them of the love of things that are not God. Such a soul, says St. Teresa, is always "fonder of spiritual sweetness than of crosses,"[13] and this fondness must be stripped for it to make progress. The wise soul who finds itself in this challenging place will yield, trust, and keep moving toward the goal. Teresa recalls the scriptural basis that signals that the only way to the center of the castle is the same path Jesus revealed: "If any man would come after me, let him deny himself and take up his cross daily and follow me. For whoever would save his life will lose it; and whoever loses his life for my sake, he will save it. For what does it profit a man if he gains the whole world and loses or forfeits himself?" (Luke 9:23–25).

So it is that this state can be a glorious waypoint on the journey if the soul holds nothing back and seeks the "complete self-renunciation" of the cross. Otherwise, St. Teresa reveals, holding on to created things will make this phase of the spiritual journey "very arduous and oppressive," rather than the liberating and freeing phase it should be.[14]

Summary of the Battles of the Third Mansion

Demonic goal: To cause discouragement in the new experience of aridity and difficulty in prayer and thereby to fight to turn the soul back to sin, worldly attachments, and the path to Hell by directly opposing every step the soul has taken toward becoming an authentic disciple of Jesus.

---

[13] *Interior Castle*, Third Mansions, chap. 1.
[14] *Interior Castle*, Third Mansions, chap. 2.

Key tactics of the enemy
- To cause discouragement and desolation due to the new experience of aridity and the consequent misunderstanding of what is happening to you when you experience contemplative aridity
- To cause or incite persecutions—criticism or attacks from others—resulting in discouragement and desolation, to motivate you to turn back
- To entice you to justify holding on to "little" or even seemingly good attachments with the rationalization that so much progress has been made (a temptation to pride) and that the attachments are harmless and present no obstacles to further growth

How to battle these tactics successfully
- You must *never* fail in your commitment to the practice of daily mental prayer, especially if you find yourself in aridity or difficulty in prayer. You must work with constant diligence to deepen your relationship with Christ in prayer and to show up, no matter how you feel. Just showing up can sometimes be the key to victory over the enemy in this phase.
- There is a wonderful saying worth remembering and reflecting on that can be helpful in this phase: "Stop holding on to things that God is trying to free you from." You are meant to fly, and God wants to cut the ties that keep you tethered to the world, the flesh, and the devil. Seek to be aware of, understand, and actively disengage when you notice even the faintest attachment to worldly goods, honor, pleasure, habits, and so forth. A note of importance here is that these attachments may also be

to certain people or relationships that, though they may not be objectively sinful, still present to you the danger of being near occasions of sin; the enemy may use these people or relationships to lure you subtly away from your good habits and growing virtue by many small steps. St. Teresa discusses this subtle and difficult problem in great detail in her autobiography as one she herself experienced early on in her journey. A contemporary example might be the friend of twenty years who does not share your Faith or life of prayer and with whom you notice a tendency in yourself to drink too much or criticize others or frequent questionable social venues. Similarly, perhaps as you experience more healing from past wounds through prayer in the heart of Christ, you discover that certain relationships cause you to sacrifice or are harmful in various ways to your dignity as a person beloved of God and that you need to detach and set hard boundaries around these relationships in order to be free to follow Christ further along the path to union with Him. Obviously, these distinctions require much attention, prayer, reflection, and counsel with a wise spiritual person or director; here, you simply want to be aware that, in this phase, all aspects of your life can present attachments from which you must choose to be untethered if you are to proceed on the way to the center of the castle. As you discover these attachments, you must aggressively seek to separate yourself from them. God will reward your efforts, and He Himself will free you from them, but your choice actively to renounce them is key.

• Carefully guard and continue to advance your spiritual progress strategically through the daily examen and your plan of love or rule of life. This daily monitoring of progress or regress helps you to fight your natural tendencies to grow complacent and rest on your progress, allowing you to stay sober and alert, on watch for the enemy who prowls around like a roaring lion, seeking some one to devour" (1 Pet. 5:8).

• Diligently seek to become more aware of your imperfections and ensure that you don't excuse or rationalize them, but instead fight them just as aggressively as you did your mortal or other habitual sins earlier on in your spiritual progress.

• Begin to identify virtues that are not yet habitual and seek to acquire them in very specific ways that you detail in your plan of love.

• Actively develop strong spiritual relationships and pray for and seek out a spiritual director or spiritual partner, or both, who can hold you accountable to your plan of love.

Spiritual encouragement: You have come a long way and should praise God and remain humbly grateful for this progress. As you do this, He will strengthen you and continue to lead you into deeper relationship with Himself.

Questions for Reflection

Review the three phases of the interior life. Where do you think you are on the spectrum of these phases? What would the holy people who are close to you say about your analysis? A very powerful exercise would be to have them read the phases of progress and tell you where they think you are.

Do you have habitual sin of any kind? If so, then you are still in the purgative way and need to make targeted plans to move beyond this place where you are straddling true life in Christ and the risk of certain death by the enemy of your soul. What can you do to fight and rid yourself of this habitual sin? If you don't know the answer, to whom can you turn for wisdom on these things? If you are seeking formation in this area, see the Resources for Continued Spiritual Growth.

When you evaluate yourself according to this continuum of spiritual progress, which areas of weakness do you find you need to focus your attention on to get stronger?

What are some things you know deep down that you are attached to and need to let go of? Whom can you talk to for help in gaining perspective on how to get these things out of your life? What are some of the difficulties or temptations you might encounter as you work toward detaching from these things?

Has the enemy attacked you and then, in the stress and desolation of it all, succeeded in enticing you to go back to your old ways? What have these temptations been? What are the tactics of the enemy that are specific to your particular struggles? How can you fight and strengthen the weak points in your character and life?

What are the specific virtues that you need to develop or strengthen? How, specifically, can you do this daily? Add these goals to your plan of love.

4

The Battles of the Fourth Mansion

Based on the troubling results of ongoing surveys of Catholic belief in recent decades, coupled with how the majority of Catholics consistently vote and behave in the cultural and political arena as well as within the Church, it is not a leap in logic to conclude that the majority of Catholics are stuck in the early purgative stage and objectively are on their way to Hell. Coupled with the teaching of Jesus that most souls are on the "wide"[15] way to destruction and the insights and observations of the spiritual Doctors of the Church, we can easily conclude that most are lost to the world, the flesh, and the devil well before reaching the illuminative phase. Why, then, should time be wasted reflecting on the wisdom of St. Teresa from here on out? The answer is that sometimes only a glimpse of the finish line, or a promise of achieving it, is needed to instill the courage to keep running the race. St. Teresa argues that if she doesn't reveal these stages of spiritual growth, then the people of God will neither aspire to nor recognize them should they receive the grace to arrive there.

---

[15] See the Gospel of Matthew chapter 7 as one of many examples.

The Devil in the Castle

As it enters the fourth mansion and beyond, the soul finds itself in rarefied air and, depending on individual circumstances, a very thinly populated place. This can lead the soul to one of the most significant challenges in this realm—loneliness. This loneliness is existential, deep, and abiding. Going deeper into the castle means leaving many things, ways of being, and even people and relationships behind. Because so few people, even generally good Catholics, understand what it means to be detached from worldly goods, to care nothing for reputation or created things, and to desire only those things that lead one to God—or even want to explore what that might mean—the soul who progresses into this mansion often feels as if it lives alone between two worlds. This is actually a state to be desired, as St. John of the Cross says that the soul should strive to live as though it were alone with God in the world. However, the reality of this state creates a painful tension for the soul and can complicate relationships with friends and family who perhaps are not on the same spiritual path or even interested in living a spiritual life. The choices and changes the soul is making in order to grow closer to God may confuse or even frustrate them. The fact remains that there is a clear choice for the soul to make here, and it is generally very challenging and sometimes painful.

There is a hidden and profoundly powerful blessing in this suffering: that this loneliness can and should lead the soul to rely on the Lord more than ever before—to share in His suffering and aloneness as the incarnate God-Man. This suffering can also motivate the soul to seek out and cherish holy relationships and faithful Catholic community. It can find encouragement in the consideration that this dwelling place is closer to God and the center of the castle and very far from where it came. The soul who reaches this point would never choose to turn back, though it might be deceived into doing so by being led astray by apparently good things it thinks are of God but are illusions of the enemy.

St. Teresa reveals that "poisonous creatures seldom enter" these sacred rooms.[16] By God's grace and the soul's efforts to detach from the world and grow in virtue, most of the handles the devil had used to grab the soul and jerk it around have dissolved. Now the soul lives apart from those manipulations related to possessions, honor, and reputation.

St. Teresa seeks to help the soul to understand that the work of those few poisonous creatures found here "do the soul good" by aiding it in its sanctification and spiritual progress.[17] This should encourage the soul to stay in the fight. Not only does the power of the enemy wane dramatically as the soul enters the realm of contemplative graces, but the presence and work of God in the soul increases dramatically as well. Joy and peace become very strong in the hearts of those so close to the King of Kings and so distant from the cares of the world. Aside from the promises of Heaven, the beauty of freedom from habitual sin and a deeper ability to hear and follow the voice of God in a place of peace should be enough to spur on even the weariest of pilgrims. Regardless, only those who keep up the fight continue to make progress.

How is it possible that the work of the devil aids the soul in this mansion? It is because the temptations bring clarity regarding the work of God in the soul. Said another way, sin no longer dominates the soul, and awareness of self and God

---

[16] *Interior Castle*, Fourth Mansions, chap. 1.
[17] *Interior Castle*, Fourth Mansions, chap. 1.

are heightened here; thus, when temptation, sin, or imperfections emerge, they serve as lights to the soul to grow in deeper Godward self-knowledge with respect to the need for deeper purifications or healing, which the soul participates in through greater ascesis (purposeful self-giving and self-denial). The importance of self-knowledge is a recurring essential theme for St. Teresa. It is a bit like a dashboard light on your car. You can cry and carry on and complain about the dashboard light out of a feeling of helplessness, or you can say, "Thank God I know about this problem so I can seek a remedy." By this phase of spiritual growth, the soul becomes very clearly aware of the way to remedy the challenge as it has a dramatically increased trust in God that gives it the strength to stay in the fight and seek ongoing healing. Teresa gives pointed assurance that the soul can and will understand itself if it makes rigorous effort, relies on the Lord, and remains steadfast in the practice of daily mental prayer.

St. Teresa similarly reveals that in this mansion, it is helpful and common for the soul to fluctuate between consolation and desolation. Why would this be the case? There are many reasons, but perhaps the most important one is to keep it awake and vigilant to the dangers surrounding it and aware of where it is in the journey to God so that it does not lose its way through complacency or distraction or subtle pride in its progress. This reality can be compared to making a long journey in a car. The monotonous buzz of the road can lull you into a state that is like being partially asleep. Then, when someone suddenly slams on his brakes in front of you, your adrenaline spikes and you are suddenly very awake and alert to what is happening. Similarly, God can permit the soul to experience trials of the enemy that can have an effect similar to that of the unexpected flare of brake lights: they serve to wake the soul up, to warn it to pay attention because of the danger around and within it, and to intensely focus on how God is leading it in the journey to Heaven.

The next avenue of demonic assault in this mansion occurs in mental prayer. The devil begins to prompt the soul to disturbance by distractions or by worrying over the way the mind wanders while in prayer. It is important to note that this disturbance comes to one who is in the illuminative way. This is an advanced soul, and it *still* deals with these disturbances. The way to combat this trouble is twofold. First, the soul should understand and accept that a wandering mind is normal and strive to be at peace about it. Second, the soul should take the single most decisive action available in this type of battle: it should just peacefully draw its attention back to the Lord in whatever manner is most helpful. For example, the soul can simply and gently whisper the name of Jesus. This serves both to draw the attention back to Him and as a means of spiritual warfare because Jesus' name is repugnant to the demons and they will often flee at the sound of it. Another approach when distracted is to offer a simple expression of love to God, such as, "I am sorry, Lord, please help me to focus on You." Another can be a simple phrase such as "I love You, Lord." Regardless of what the phrase is, the point is simply to draw the heart and mind, in a very peaceful way, back to God.

Distractions in prayer can come from two main sources: the devil and weaknesses in the soul itself. (Obviously, there are environmental distractions, but these are not what St. Teresa is referring to.) If the devil is the cause of the distractions, then they will cease with God's intervention. The soul can have some reasonable certainty that the enemy is the cause if the soul deals with the distraction through spiritual warfare, such as saying the name of Jesus or praying the St. Michael prayer, and the results are clear and immediate. If the enemy is not the source of the distractions, then the wandering may continue, and the soul should give no attention to it in terms of getting frustrated. The key is to remain at peace in this process and not to give in to agitation, self-reproach, or frustration or, worse, cut short the time allotted to prayer. The demon can use the distractions to trick the soul into any one of these harmful actions. Frustration rooted in the soul's unreasonable expectations about its own capabilities or how holy it is or how well it should be able to pray now that it has achieved this level of progress can and will place it back into the enemy's control because this kind of frustration is most often rooted in pride.

Regardless of the source of distractions, the struggle against them is all a great burden to the soul. St. Teresa notes that "most of these trials and times of unrest come from the fact that we do not understand ourselves."[18] Even so, she describes the trials as necessary for the soul's sanctification. The soul must endure and engage the spiritual warfare and deepen its insight into its human weaknesses and how little it is capable of without God's help. The soul must gently fight and endure but must not become frustrated. This is accomplished through realistic expectations and trust in the One who knows of the soul's weaknesses and desires to heal it and promises to do so, as long as the soul stays in the fight by cooperating with Him. The distractions, then, are one way in which the devil actually aids the soul's spiritual progress in this mansion and why God permits his activity here. With the proper perspective, it is clear to see that God allows

---

[18] *Interior Castle*, Fourth Mansions, chap. 1.

these distractions to strengthen the soul and deepen its trust in God. The key is to remain at peace and bring the gaze of the mind and heart gently back to Jesus, who alone is the author of all the soul's prayer.

In this fourth mansion St. Teresa warns the soul diligently to avoid two things. The first is the near occasion of sin, and the second is the cessation or pausing of mental prayer for any reason. The near occasion of sin can be understood as any person, place, or thing that, of its nature or because of human frailty, can lead one to commit sin. The reason is obvious on its face. If the soul truly desires never to offend God or to sin, it will diligently, consistently, and purposefully orient its life in such a way that it never even comes close to those things that tempt it or allow it proximity to whatever leads it to sin.

Here is a good way of thinking about this. If you have a sin that you easily fall into, think of that sin at the center of a target. The ring closest to the center we can call the NO Zone (Near Occasion Zone). You know that if you dip into the NO Zone, you are very likely to be carried into the sin itself. It is a bit like two powerful magnets. One is a sin magnet at the center of the target. That sin magnet is attracted to a magnet in you that is made up of patterns of sin and related weakness of the will, or concupiscence. When you get into the NO Zone, the magnets are close enough together to be drawn to each other inevitably and with great force, and then you find yourself in sin. So the diligent avoidance of the near occasion is to understand and recognize the NO Zone and then avoid that area as if it were mortal sin itself. For example, if you know that you have a problem with porn and that this problem surfaces when you are tired, and the NO Zone is any computer activity, then you would purposefully stay completely away from your computer when you are tired. This plan of action keeps you out of the NO Zone and thus out of sin.[19]

Beyond the importance of avoiding the near occasion of sin, St. Teresa argues that the devil desires even more keenly to win the soul over because, at this stage, the soul is very attractive to others and often influences others to follow God. She reflects that if the soul makes it this far and then falls into sin and public scandal, much is lost in the soul's case and much is gained by the devil. Care for the spiritual well-being of those entrusted to the soul at this stage can be a great motivator to stay out of the NO Zone. Teresa also argues that remaining dedicated to prayer is a powerful protection against falling into sin because it increases the soul's awareness of its tendency to sin through its own weaknesses and its awareness of all the other factors of its life that, if ignored, would allow it easily to fall into sin. Put another way, mental prayer increases self-awareness, increases love for God and neighbor, and thus works as a powerful deterrent against sin by increasing the virtues in the soul.

One of the dangers to the devout soul who remains steadfast in its commitment to prayer is that the devil can provide a counterfeit experience of prayer that in some way mirrors Teresa's description of the movements of God. She admonishes us to recognize the fruits of authentic prayer as the primary measure of whether the experiences of prayer are from God. If the fruit of prayer is growth in humility, love of God, deepening growth in the virtues, and other expressions of charity, the likelihood of counterfeit experiences is far less since experiences from the devil cannot bring lasting good fruit and ultimately create disquiet, a

[19] For a free course on the NO Zone and on overcoming habitual sin, go to ApostoliViae.org.

loss of peace, or some other diminishment or disturbance in the soul and its good habits.

Summary of the Battles of the Fourth Mansion

Demonic goal: The goal remains to dissuade you from continuing the journey deeper into the castle. However, the tactics shift to temptations to frustration regarding experiences in prayer and efforts to lure you into near occasions of sin and to get you to give up the practice of daily mental prayer.

Key tactics of the enemy
- To tempt you to sin or imperfections
- To disturb or worry you about how your mind wanders in prayer

How to battle these tactics successfully
- Recognize that temptations at this stage shed light on the need for deeper healing and growth in self-awareness.
- Be encouraged that God is revealing your sinful tendencies and areas in your soul where you need healing or greater maturity.
- Pay diligent attention to these temptations to understand better what God is doing and where and how you need healing.
- Avoid a prideful assessment of failure when your mind wanders, as if you could control your mind if you simply worked harder. Simply ignore and avoid making a fuss over your wandering mind.
- When your mind wanders in prayer, gently and peacefully turn your attention back to the Lord through a simple prayer or by repeating the name of Jesus.

The Devil in the Castle

- Expect that your mind will wander in prayer unless God intervenes. Be at peace with this reality and the truth of your weaknesses when left without God's help, so that the challenge of distractions can become an opportunity for growth in humility and trust in the Lord.
- Never, ever, for any reason, abandon the practice of daily mental prayer.

Spiritual encouragement: The enemy's power over you is weakening in dramatic fashion. Even temptations are allowed to lead you to healing and an awareness of the truth that God desires to purify you more deeply so that He might draw you closer to Himself.

Questions for Reflection

Have you noticed the reduced power of temptation at this point in your journey?

- *If not, how can you fight more specifically against sin and temptation? You might look at the Resources for Continued Spiritual Growth for ways you can grow spiritually, or consider taking the free Overcoming Habitual Sin course at ApostoliViae.org.*

- *If you have noticed a reduced power of temptation, how can you focus in on what your temptations lead to with respect to healing, purification, and deeper union with God?*

Do you struggle with frustration about distractions of the mind in prayer? If so, consider how you can apply St. Teresa's wisdom on how to deal with these distractions rooted in:

• *Demonic temptations: What spiritual-warfare tactics can you adopt?*

• *Your own weaknesses: How can you deal with moments of distraction rooted in your humanity?*

5

The Battles of the Fifth Mansion

On entering this mansion, our habited holy guide pauses to pray for us. "Send me light from Heaven, my Lord, that I may enlighten these Thy servants, to some of whom Thou art often pleased to grant fruition of these joys, lest, when the devil transfigures himself into an angel of light, he should deceive them, for all their desires are occupied in desiring to please Thee."[20]

As she reveals in her prayer, the devil in these later stages poses as an "angel of light." Why does the devil pose as an angel of light, and what does this mean? Simply put, at this stage of maturity, the soul is not likely to fall due to temptations to mortal or grave sins. It will generally be cautious against even venial sins and will have made much effort to detach from the things of the world that qualify as NO Zones. Instead, in these mansions, the soul is tempted to things that are actual or perceived goods but still are either not of God or not God's will for the soul. An actual good can be bad when it distracts the soul from God's central call or purpose.

[20] *Interior Castle*, Fifth Mansions, chap. 1.

For example, a person of goodwill who truly seeks to follow God's will can be tempted to take on too many good projects—to the point at which it disrupts her family life or her health. As an example, a devout Catholic woman was once asked to assist the diocesan exorcist during his sessions. She called me to ask whether this was wise. Given that she has a number of children who are teens and pre-teens, we determined that while this would indeed be a good thing to assist the priest with, it would be a potential nightmare for the family if they experienced spiritual retaliation because of her service. Another example might be a father who has a young teenage boy who seems to be straying from the Faith and virtue. The father is simultaneously asked to lead a men's group at his parish. A choice to serve the men's group, objectively a very good thing, would be a very bad move at this time because it would allow the enemy to distract him away from focusing more attention on his son when he needs it most.

As to perceived goods that are not actual goods, these can be deceptions that masquerade as experiences or revelations from God but are actually from the devil. For example, a devout Catholic woman in a difficult marriage heard in prayer what she thought was God's call to leave her marriage and become a nun. Although becoming a nun is a very good thing objectively, one cannot abandon a valid sacramental marriage in order to enter the convent. In this case, the inspiration was a demonic impulse that played upon the woman's suffering. The woman received good counsel and stayed in her marriage. By God's grace, things eventually improved, and she was grateful she did not follow that impulse. Another example is of a man who had made great progress in his spiritual life that caused tension and distance between him and his wife. This tension and his real desire for union with

God led him to conclude that he needed to spend time daily at his parish in eucharistic adoration. The time he spent, coupled with the commute to and from the church, created a significant period of absence from his wife. This caused even more damage to the relationship and made it clear that this was not a decision rooted in sound discernment.

There are countless examples of this kind of deception, and it is not possible to cover all the angles. As St. Teresa reveals, though the lizards in this stage are few, they tend to be more "agile" and are better able to hide, deceive, and disguise their intentions to harm the soul. These now appear cloaked in light, as apparently good and worthy options that God may be asking the soul to pursue, when, in reality, they lead the soul far from the path God has set it on and end up placing it in darkness. A key antidote to this serious battle is a relationship with an experienced spiritual director who can help the soul better evaluate and understand the movements of God and the enemy in this stage of its growth.

St. Teresa notes that the enemy can also cause the soul to enter into a kind of mystical state that it might interpret as from God but is not from God. The way to discern the difference involves several aspects of what is described as a kind of rapture. Rather than focus excessively on the false variations of this experience, St. Teresa reveals the characteristics of an authentic contemplative encounter with God:

1. When God draws the soul into this experience, it can neither see, hear, nor understand what is happening.
2. This kind of experience is always very short in duration.
3. There are no lasting thoughts associated with this encounter.

4. Here the soul experiences joy that is beyond all joys and nothing like anything ever experienced in the normal course of the blessings of life.

5. The soul is unable to doubt that the encounter was from God and is absolutely certain of this even after a long period of time has passed since the experience occurred.

6. The union comes following no effort of the soul, but only that of God. In fact, Teresa emphasizes that the soul can only prepare for the graces of contemplation but cannot produce them through any acts of its own. This fact also protects the soul from deception in that, if it somehow can produce some kind of related phenomenon by its own actions, it can know it is not from the Lord. This is a particularly important point, as many in the Centering Prayer movement teach that a particular approach to prayer can produce contemplative prayer.[21]

Our great saint concludes this explanation with an admonition to humility: "What a lot we shall see if we desire to see no more than our own baseness and wretchedness and to understand that we are not worthy to be the handmaidens of so great a Lord, since we cannot comprehend His marvels. May He be forever praised. Amen."[22]

St. Teresa then reveals a truth that is very difficult to understand for the soul who has not yet entered into this level of

---

[21] The best resource on this topic is Connie Rossini's book *Is Centering Prayer Catholic?* Visit https://contemplativehomeschool. com/product/is-centering-prayer-catholic/.

[22] *Interior Castle*, Fifth Mansions, chap. 1.

sanctity. She reveals that the devil "gives a false and short-lived peace to the soul in order later to wage a far severer war upon it."[23] This makes sense when we consider that Jesus promises His peace to those who seek Him and dwell with Him. The devil can provide a counterfeit experience of peace to draw the soul aside from the hard work of authentic discipleship, to entice it to rest and enjoy the fruits of "peace" after its long labors, thus blinding it to the false nature of the peace he is offering and luring it step by step out of the narrow way and onto the broad road to Hell.

It is unfortunate that one of the most common false teachings in the Church (even among faithful Catholics) is that if a person has peace, he is in God's will or in a good place spiritually. It is very common to hear people offer the advice: "If you have peace in your decision, then it is the right decision." The only way to determine if peace is an indication of God's will or blessings is to know the entire context of a person's spiritual life. This cannot be emphasized enough. All those who give this advice should simply cease to do so and instead begin to study Ignatian discernment of spirits, both first and second rules, begin to practice them diligently in daily life according to their spiritual progress, and study the writings of St. John of the Cross. Most who give this bad advice will end up in a Confession line after even a cursory study of key resources provided in the recommended reading at the end of this book. To go into the deep waters of this topic is beyond the scope of the present work but is essential, long-term formation for the soul who is serious about the spiritual journey.[24]

---

[23] *Interior Castle*, Fifth Mansions, chap. 2.

[24] The best starting point for understanding this topic is my book *Spiritual Warfare and the Discernment of Spirits*.

The Devil in the Castle

St. Teresa specifically mentions and strongly asserts the warning offered above: that the soul in these mansions must commit to proper, ordered formation in the discernment of spirits, along with steadfast mental prayer, explored in detail by St. Ignatius of Loyola in his second set of rules for those beyond the purgative way.[25] The Carmelites of St. Teresa's time were greatly aided by faithful, learned, experienced Jesuit spiritual directors, and she likely learned this from them and from her own experience. In fact, the way she words her concerns sounds very much like St. Ignatius when he warns of a peace that begins well and ends poorly. For the purposes of the discussion of the soul's experience of the enemy in this mansion, it is enough to say that when the soul has peace and discerns a path forward based on that peace, it needs to keep a close eye on how things unfold until it can, in fact, verify that it is on the right path. The way the soul knows it is on the path God wills for it is that what begins in virtue

---

[25] It is assumed that the soul will have first assimilated, through much study and long practice, the first set of rules for the discernment of spirits as defined by St. Ignatius. It is vital that, in order to avoid profound confusion, the reader who is unfamiliar with the topic of discernment of spirits should study and then practice the discernment of spirits in the order that St. Ignatius provided them. It is beyond the scope and purpose of this book to explore this topic other than emphatically stating the essential necessity of the rules and the need to follow them exactly as Ignatius lays them out for each spiritual situation. These situations can be seen to correspond quite clearly to Teresa's mansions and the various ways of spiritual progress discussed in chapter 3, on the third mansions. The first step, as indicated above, is to read and then begin the daily practice of discernment of spirits guidance offered in *Spiritual Warfare and the Discernment of Spirits*. This study, coupled with daily mental prayer for at least several years, will be vital to avoiding confusion and gaining understanding of the topic outlined above.

remains in virtue and ends in virtue. False peace in the realm of the soul beyond habitual sin often begins with peace and then slowly veers off track, and the soul finds itself in a place that is not intended or desired by God or itself, either in temptation against virtues already acquired or actually falling into sin, or else being disquieted or anxious, worried or mistrustful. These are all clear signs of the presence of the enemy.

St. Teresa writes, "The wiles of the devil are terrible; he will run a thousand times around hell if by so doing he can make us believe that we have a single virtue which we have not."[26] The unfortunate reality is that the human person has an infinite capacity for self-deception. Even this far into the castle, Teresa reveals, the soul can believe it loves God with all it is and actually still live in some ways that contradict that belief. St. Teresa challenges the soul to proceed with caution and concludes that, though it cannot know if it truly loves God in a perfect sense, the soul can know the fruits of what it means to love its neighbor. And if the soul does truly love its neighbor, then it is evident that it does, in fact, love God. One of the many ways to determine this is for the soul to assess its patience with others. Another is for the soul to examine its life against the fruits of the Holy Spirit revealed by St. Paul in Galatians 5:22–23: Does it act with increasing evidence of "love, joy, peace, patience, kindness, goodness, faithfulness, gentleness, self-control" in the events of its daily life? These fruits are evidence of God's work in the soul; evidence of the opposite is a sign that the soul needs to reevaluate how it is living and the choices it is making, even if those seem to be objectively good choices.

Authentic love can be challenging to understand and live out in difficult circumstances, especially in a culture and time in

---

[26] *Interior Castle*, Fifth Mansions, chap. 3.

which the very definition of love has been deformed and is no longer understood. In our time, there is much shouting, complaining, and frustration among the laity over the grave sins of the clergy. It is often said that "love is telling the truth." This is true, but it is a very small slice of the greater whole of what it means to love as Jesus loved. As an example, St. Teresa warns that there is a lack of love when the soul is prideful and has a critical spirit, "even if only in small things," concerning its neighbor.[27] If the soul tells the truth in a way that is prideful, its act of "love" is tainted by something contrary to it. So, although telling the truth is clearly one aspect of an expression of love, doing so in a manner that lacks gentleness and reverence for the soul of the recipient is not an act of love but is instead tainted and destructive. This requisite gentleness and respect in expressing the truth as a charitable act must not be seen as a vapid "church of nice" sentiment but, instead, as the clear guidance of the Holy Spirit.

Here are a few verses in the New Testament that reveal the call of the Holy Spirit regarding how the soul should treat those it claims to love. In each verse, the fruit of charity—the particular virtue or behavioral trait—is italicized. These verses are followed by helpful prompts (also in italics) to serve as a reflective self-examen regarding how these admonitions manifest or fail to manifest themselves in the daily life of the soul. True love of neighbor will directly manifest itself in observable behavior that stands the test of these admonitions:

And we exhort you, brethren, admonish the idle, encourage the fainthearted, help the weak, be *patient* with them all. (1 Thess. 5:14)

---

[27] *Interior Castle*, Fifth Mansions, chap. 3.

Am I patient and self-sacrificing with those who need to hear the truth?

Therefore, be alert, remembering that for three years I did not cease night or day to admonish every one with *tears.* (Acts 20:31)

Does my passion for God come through humble tears of love as I communicate truth, or am I cold, demanding, and dispassionate, as were many of the Pharisees whom Jesus railed against?

Let your speech always be *gracious*, seasoned with salt, so that you may know how you ought to answer every one. (Col. 4:6)

Am I gracious and careful regarding how I prepare the meal of truth? Is my meal stark and made up merely of sound nutrients, or does it mirror the banquet feast of God that is both nutritious and so appealing that none would turn away to a lesser source? Is my approach to telling the truth winning to those with whom I disagree, or is it appealing only to those who already agree with me?

And the Lord's servant must not be quarrelsome but kindly to every one, an apt teacher, forbearing, correcting his opponents with *gentleness.* God may perhaps grant that they will repent and come to know the truth, and they may escape from the snare of the devil, after being captured by him to do his will. (2 Tim. 2:24–26)

Am I quick to argue and defend without the patience that reflects kindness? Or am I gentle and hopeful, relying on the work of God that comes through the authentic and self-giving expression of love and truth?

Remind them ... to *speak evil of no one, to avoid quarreling, to be gentle,* and to *show perfect courtesy* toward all men. (Titus 3:1–2)

Do I speak poorly of those who are deceived and in need of the light and the work of redemption? Or am I courteous, and do I avoid a confrontational stance that will easily lead to closed hearts and minds? Do I treat communication of truth as a boxing match or as a sharing of love between friends?

He can deal *gently* with the ignorant and wayward, since he himself is beset with weakness. (Heb. 5:2)

Do I recognize my own weakness and sin in humility as I work to help others, or do I place myself above others as the one who is right and superior? Am I ready to wash the feet of the wayward, as Jesus did with Judas, or do I stand above God Himself in my refusal of humble service based on the fact that others are broken and in sin?

But the wisdom from above is first pure, then *peaceable, gentle, open to reason, full of mercy* and good fruits, without uncertainty or insincerity. (Jas. 3:17)

Am I peaceful, gentle, and open to discussion with others? Or am I hard and quick to shut down anything that I disagree with without hearing the heart of others? Am I constantly waiting to get to my retort, or do I truly care enough about the hearts of others to listen carefully so that I can reach their hearts with the truths that would most likely set them free? Am I just interested in winning the argument?

But in your hearts reverence Christ as Lord. Always be prepared to make a defense to anyone who calls you to account for the hope that is in you, yet do it with *gentleness* and *reverence.* (1 Pet. 3:15)

Am I prepared to reveal gently and reverently what God has done and is doing in my life? Am I deeply aware of my own need for a Savior and thus recognize and long for the salvation of others? Have I prayed for the one I am seeking to help? Am I in a state of grace so that I am animated by God's love, gentleness, meekness, and power as I speak?

One of the names God has given the devil is "accuser of the brethren" (see Rev. 12:10). The soul who truly longs to be one with the Lord must not be an accuser but must be instead one who walks with the broken, in a spirit of truth and charity, and helps them to wholeness and holiness. St. Teresa exhorts that "when we see a fault in someone, we should be as sorry about it as if it were our own and try to conceal it from others."[28] This, of course, does not include grave sins, such as abuse, which should always be dealt with and exposed, but it does include all things short of this level of gravity that the soul encounters as it seeks to follow the Lord. When Teresa speaks of concealing the faults of others, it may sound initially as if she is speaking of covering sin or denying the truth about behaviors that cause harm. But she intends something quite different here. For example, let's say someone was brought up in a very abusive environment and, though he is trying to follow Jesus, he tends to speak in ways often contrary to what is outlined above. Should the soul condemn that person and separate itself from him, or should the soul instead overlook the person's challenging behaviors, remember its own faltering steps toward acquiring virtue and its need of grace, and try gently to coach that person when it finds an opening? Clearly, prudence and discernment are necessary here, especially if there

---

[28] *Interior Castle*, Fifth Mansions, chap. 3.

are proximate physical, spiritual, or moral dangers. But Teresa's point is that of the Gospel: Jesus exhorts against hypocrisy and a critical spirit regarding one's neighbor when He says, "First take the log out of your own eye, and then you will see clearly to take the speck out of your brother's eye" (Matt. 7:5). Until the soul has examined itself and its own life in the Lord, as facilitated, for example, by the Scripture verses and reflection questions above, it needs to proceed with great caution when speaking to another soul about its faults and sins and should refrain from publicizing these to others, which happens all too often today. The soul on the journey to God would not want its faults exposed and spotlighted; neither should it expose its neighbor to that kind of treatment. It should instead, as Teresa suggests, proceed with care and delicacy to cover its neighbor's faults as with a veil, remembering its own weaknesses, and work to assume the best of its neighbor, for it cannot know the efforts and wounds within the heart of its neighbor nor judge its neighbor's sincerity before God. When the soul takes this kind of approach to living in and speaking the truth, it does so in the recognition that all are broken and sinful and in need of supportive, compassionate, patient, and kind companions along the way to union with God.

As the great mystical Doctor draws her tour of the fifth mansion to a close, she returns to a previous concern and reminds the soul to take great caution against even the near occasion of sin. She notes that "even in this state the soul is not strong enough to be able to run into them safely."[29] She means that the soul must not run into or through the realm of the near occasion of sin, the NO Zone, as was discussed previously. This is quite a remarkable statement, as the soul in this realm is well beyond habitual sin

---

[29] *Interior Castle*, Fifth Mansions, chap. 4.

of any kind and likely confirmed in the illuminative way. St. Teresa gives this warning because the enemy steps up his assault to ensure that the soul does not enter further into the castle, to approach the heights of union that the Lord desires to bring it to. The soul might ask why the enemy mounts an increased assault in this mansion. The reason is that, once it has progressed into this deeper state of union with God, the soul is completely surrendered to God, and any battles with the devil in this realm leave the enemy battered and bruised. St. Teresa is so concerned that advanced souls not grow complacent or presumptuous of assured victory that she warns:

> I tell you, daughters, I have known people of a very high degree of spirituality who have reached this state, and whom, notwithstanding, the devil, with great subtlety and craft, has won back to himself. For this purpose, he will marshal all the powers of hell, for, as I have often said, if he wins a single soul in this way he will win a whole multitude.[30]

This warning should give the soul great pause for reflection as it recalls that its life of sanctity will draw many others to God along with it, but if it falls away in this place through the devil's wiles, it will also draw with it those it was meant to help bring to Christ. This shows the crucial importance and role of even one soul committed to following the path to the heart of the castle and how it might impact other souls for good or ill, depending on how, or if, it proceeds. Although the enemy might change his tactics and although the soul in this mansion has left grave and venial sin behind, the battle against sin and concupiscence will

---

[30] *Interior Castle*, Fifth Mansions, chap. 4.

never leave it until the minute God takes it from this exile to Himself. Even imperfections at this stage (the final inclinations of lesser love) can and will hinder the soul's progress further into the castle; the soul must continue to be alert and watchful because the enemy will use anything to erect an obstacle to advancement.

St. Teresa asks two very important and pointed questions related to this crucial spiritual battle before providing a single answer that addresses them both. These questions are worth reflecting on regarding self-perception and spiritual progress:

1. If the soul is so completely at one with the will of God, as has been said, how can it be deceived, since it never desires to follow its own will?[31]

2. By what avenues can the devil enter and lead you into such peril that your soul may be lost, when you are so completely withdrawn from the world and so often approach the Sacraments? For you are enjoying the companionship, as we might say, of angels, since, by the goodness of the Lord, you have none of you any other desires than to serve and please Him in everything. It would not be surprising, you might add, if this should happen to those who are immersed in the cares of the world.[32]

The answer: The devil, under the guise of "doing good, sets about undermining [the soul] in trivial ways, and involving it in practices which, so he gives it to understand, are not wrong; little by little he darkens its understanding, and weakens its will, and causes its self-love to increase, until

---

[31] *Interior Castle*, Fifth Mansions, chap. 4.
[32] *Interior Castle*, Fifth Mansions, chap. 4.

in one way and another he begins to withdraw it from the love of God and to persuade it to indulge its own wishes."[33]

St. Teresa then shares her wisdom on how to fight this deception:

We must continually ask God in our prayers to keep us in His hand, and bear constantly in mind that, if He leaves us, we shall at once be down in the depths, as indeed we shall. So we must never have any confidence in ourselves—that would simply be folly. But most of all we must walk with special care and attention, and watch what progress we make in the virtues, and discover if, in any way, we are either improving or going back, especially in our love for each other and in our desire to be thought least of, and in ordinary things; for if we look to this, and beg the Lord to give us light, we shall at once discern whether we have gained or lost.[34]

Once again, the integral need for humility and Godward self-awareness is emphasized. This was the theme at the entrance into the castle, and it continues throughout the journey; these two focal points are indispensable weapons against the enemy and must always be the first used in any spiritual battle. These weapons can be gained and used with increasing facility and discipline only through prayer and rigorous examination. The soul must constantly ask, "Am I making progress in virtue?" Even more powerfully, the soul needs to ask this of those who are closest to it and who see it in its strengths and weaknesses and so can give

---

[33] *Interior Castle*, Fifth Mansions, chap. 4.
[34] *Interior Castle*, Fifth Mansions, chap. 4.

an honest assessment. This accountability to one's neighbor is another exercise in humility and cultivates a sincerity of heart in seeking God in truth.

This is why it is vital that the soul, no matter how deeply it grows in intimacy with God, remains faithful to ascesis—deliberate self-giving and self-denial. It does this through living out a specific rule of life that it follows daily, so that it remains faithful to prayer, the examen, and the sacraments in this context. As well, Catholic community is vital to this constant challenge with self-delusion. When the soul lives an ascetical and disciplined life in community, it is always faced with challenges and opportunities for accountability. These help to ensure that the soul's compass stays on true north and the soul stays on track. It is clear that, without community, ascesis, and accountability, the soul will lose its way. St. Teresa and her primary audience lived in community together and already practiced all of these spiritual exercises, and still she reminds them that they are susceptible to this kind of subtle deception of the enemy.

The soul can never fail to be vigilant until the time comes to see God face-to-face. No matter how much progress it makes, it can never be lax in its self-evaluation and in getting feedback from others on the same. It is far too easy to be deluded and led astray—even for the most advanced souls. St. Teresa reiterates this essential truth before moving into the next mansion:

> We must strive all the time to advance, and, if we are not advancing, we must walk with great fear, as the devil is undoubtedly anxious to exercise his wiles upon us. For it is unthinkable that a soul which has arrived so far should cease to grow: love is never idle, so failure to advance would be a very bad sign. A soul which has once set out

to be the bride of God Himself, and has already had converse with His Majesty and reached the point which has been described, must not lie down and go to sleep again.[35]

In fact, these advanced souls, because their virtue is so objectively obvious to themselves and others, need to surround themselves with people who will be honest and clear about the shortcomings they see or experience. Without this serious interior work and external feedback, the soul is more likely to be self-deluded and led astray by the enemy's subtle tactics in this mansion.

Summary of the Battles of the Fifth Mansion

Demonic goal: To delude and distract you so that either your progress is hindered or you are led off the path toward union with God.

Key tactics of the enemy

- To tempt you to objectively good things that nevertheless are not of God and that will distract you from other good things that are from God and are His will for your life
- To draw you into criticism of or harshness with others
- To entice you to self-satisfaction regarding your progress
- To tempt you to confidence in your self-perception and thus a lack of humility

How to battle these tactics successfully

- Practice daily mental prayer; it is a must to keep you close to the One who reveals all.
- Participate regularly in the sacraments to nourish in you the life of God.

---

[35] *Interior Castle*, Fifth Mansions, chap. 4.

- If you have not already done so, develop a clear rule of life or plan of love that will give you a sound compass against which always to judge your progress or regress through the examen.
- Be faithful to your daily examen to keep you awake as to whether you are making specific progress against imperfections and growing in virtue.
- Get involved in healthy Catholic community and deepen your relationships with those who will keep you honest about your progress or lack thereof.

Spiritual encouragement: Those who reach this stage have been shown a "great mercy" by God. The devil's "surprises and deceptions" can be avoided by study and learning about the interior life and putting what is learned into practice. As well, God is so "anxious" for the soul "not to be lost" "that He gives it a thousand interior warnings of many kinds, and thus it cannot fail to perceive the danger."[36]

Questions for Reflection

Have you noticed any emergence of a critical spirit in you as you progress in virtue? How specifically can you put a stop to this?

Do you have a rule of life yet? Is now a good time to establish a daily specific written plan

---

[36] *Interior Castle*, Fifth Mansions, chap. 4.

regarding how you will love God and serve others?
If not, what can you do to get one in place?

Do you practice a daily examen against that rule of
life? If not, what can you do to begin this practice?

Are you involved in a community that provides structure
and accountability on this journey to God? If not, what
do you plan to do to find and get involved in one?

Would the people who know you best say that
you have grown in love and virtue in this past
year? If you don't know, what is your plan to
find out? What will you do if you discover the
answer is not as positive as you would like?

How have you sensed God's warnings and
encouragements? What have you done in response?

To find support concerning many of these questions, see the
Resources for Continued Spiritual Growth.

6

The Battles of the Sixth Mansion

The trials in the sixth mansion are many and great, but relatively few emanate directly from demonic influence. Teresa reveals that, at this point, the demons cannot, through exterior trials "inhibit the working of the faculties" or "disturb the soul in the way already described" in previous chapters.[37] The primary reason for this is that the soul is further from sin and attachments and closer to God.

In this mansion, though, St. Teresa describes a potential challenge the soul may experience with locutions. Locutions are supernatural affirmations or statements that a soul perceives in some way. These are hard to describe for the soul that has not experienced them. As an example, a holy woman was doing the dishes one day and thinking about her roles in life. She was musing, in particular, about her role as a Catholic school principal; she thought of that role as a vocation. Immediately she heard an interior voice that was not her own say, "Being a principal is not your vocation." The voice was internal, but it

[37] *Interior Castle*, Sixth Mansions, chap. 1.

wasn't her own. She then had a visual idea presented to her that basically contrasted the way she had seen all of her roles—wife, mother, principal, daughter, child of God ... —each in a box organized horizontally in the air. Then the vision shifted the boxes, and at the top was child of God; second, spouse; third, mother, and so forth. This encounter came just as she needed to make a very important decision in her life, and it helped her with great clarity to understand the decision she should make. She realized that she was trying to juggle things that were not in their proper order instead of prioritizing her energy and focus according to God's design. The locution, or what she heard and even saw, helped her on the path toward God and His will for her in a very evident way.

While this is a positive example, St. Teresa notes that locutions may originate from several places: (1) from the mind of the soul itself, (2) from God Himself, directly or through His messengers (i.e., angels), or (3) from the devil. If the locution is from God (what is called "authentic"), Teresa says it is given "for your own benefit, to comfort you or to warn you of your faults."[38] She attempts several times to list the ways to determine the authenticity of locutions and struggles to achieve an effective coherence because the nuances and circumstances involved in individual souls create some challenges here. To aid you in navigating the challenges of this mansion, I have consolidated St. Teresa's wisdom into a single complete list wherein she reveals eleven ways to test these occurrences. Also, it should be noted that locutions are not strictly limited to those souls who find themselves in the sixth mansion, though at this realm of maturity, they may be more common.

---

[38] *Interior Castle*, Sixth Mansions, chap. 3.

Testing the Authenticity of Locutions according to St. Teresa

Test 1: Regardless of the soul's inclinations or natural instincts, locutions should never be accepted on face value, but instead should always be tested to see if they agree "strictly with the Scriptures."[39] This is what Scripture and the mystics call "discernment of spirits," which was referenced in the last mansion as a crucial weapon for the journey into the castle. (Again, it cannot be emphasized enough how essential formation in discernment of spirits is for souls serious about progressing on the spiritual journey, especially in our time, when it is a great challenge to find a spiritual director who is both well formed and experienced.) Of course, this test would also apply to the authentic Magisterium of the Church, as St. Teresa describes herself as a "daughter of the Church" and states clearly that if anything that she says is found to be contrary to Church teaching it should be rejected. She also reveals, with respect to judging authenticity, that it doesn't matter whether these locutions are heard externally (as with an audible sound) or internally (in the mind or the imagination).

Test 2: The locution will immediately bring the effect that it proclaims. For example, if the soul is experiencing fear and related anxiety, and the locution "Be not afraid" is heard, an immediate and lasting calm will come over the soul.

Test 3: If the locution is accompanied by a deep peace and tranquility of soul, and the soul is thereby drawn to offer praise or thanksgiving to God, this speaks to its authenticity. This Godward orientation of the soul, inspired by the locution, is not likely caused by the enemy, as he never desires the soul to draw near to

---

[39] All of the quotations in this section on the tests are taken from *Interior Castle*, Sixth Mansions, chap. 3.

God or to praise Him unless it is a tactic used to draw the soul in a way that conflicts with the duties of the soul's state in life.

Test 4: Observe whether the words of the locution vanish from the memory quickly, or if they remain with great certainty, clarity, and strength of impression for some time, or if they never fade from memory at all. St. Teresa explains that they make such an impression on the soul "that, although sometimes they seem quite impossible of fulfilment, and we cannot help wondering if they will come true or not, and although our understanding may hesitate about it, yet within the soul itself there is a certainty which cannot be overcome." She continues that it even may seem that all is coming against what the soul heard, but the soul never wavers in faith in what it heard. This space provides a point of entry for the devil, for in the midst of this authentic locution and related certainty, the enemy tries to get the soul to doubt. The doubting is aimed at weakening the soul's conviction that God can and will do something that is beyond its comprehension or understanding regarding how the thing will be accomplished or come about. Even so, if the locution is authentic, the "spark of certainty" cannot "fail to remain alive even if the soul wished it to die." She continues, "If the locutions come from the imagination, none of these signs occur, nor is there any certainty or peace or interior consolation." Teresa notes that even if the imaginative locutions accompany authentic mystical experiences in prayer, the soul should not be deceived by them. It is very difficult to gain clarity on these experiences without a relationship with a knowledgeable and experienced spiritual director. As well, at this stage in spiritual maturity, the soul is very humble. The certainty it feels is not a stubbornness due to pride or vanity. A good test for a soul who seems to have locutions and is firm about their origin is when a spiritual director asks it to set the locution aside, ignore it, and move on. If the soul won't obey a sound spiritual director or adviser, pride is a serious problem, and as the locution seems to have created a disordered attachment, it may very likely be a counterfeit from the devil.

Test 5: If a locution is extremely clear, it is likely authentic. St. Teresa posits that this clarity "inhibits all other thoughts and compels attention to what He says" and that the Lord "can still the faculties and all the interior part of the soul in such a way that the soul becomes fully aware that another Lord, greater than itself, is governing that Castle and renders Him the greatest devotion and humility. So, it cannot do other than listen: it has no other choice." St. Teresa contrasts this with ways to test false locutions, which are not clear: the words are less distinct, and they "will be like something heard in a half-dream." She warns that while the devil can pronounce his words very clearly, he cannot replicate the other positive effects revealed in these tests, and his locutions will leave the soul restless and in turmoil rather than in peace.

Test 6: It is possible that the locution is authentic if the soul had not been thinking about the subject revealed by the locution when it occurs. More certainty can be had if the soul had never considered the idea for any reason or in any context before. This would relieve the soul of any concern that it could have been conjured up by the imagination or memory. Teresa elaborates, "The soul cannot be deceived about things it has not desired or wished for or that have never been brought to its notice." St. Ignatius elaborates more fully on this point of discernment in his rules for discerning the authenticity of spiritual inspirations and consolation. He reveals that if the inspiration has no prior cause, it is more likely from God. For example, if a young man is gardening and thinking only about gardening, and he has never thought about the priesthood before, and he hears a locution that the Lord is calling him to the priesthood, this is something he should most definitely talk with his spiritual director about.

Test 7: With "genuine locutions the soul seems to be hearing something, whereas in locutions invented by the imagination, someone seems to be composing bit by bit what the soul wishes to hear." In this case, the soul might imagine the experience of the locution as a partial idea coming to the fore and then developing piece by piece in a haphazard or forced way, or a way that plays on the imagination and then builds from there. As an example, a person watched a documentary about the challenges with clean water in Africa. The person then began to do his chores around the house and heard, "You should do something to help with water in Africa." Then he began to muse on the idea, and it turned into the need to start a nonprofit to raise funding, and so on and so on. Subsequently, the soul concluded that God told him to start a nonprofit to raise money to purify water in Africa. All this emerged because he simply may have had compassion in the first place and then constructed the plan based on his own machinations. Beyond the basics in this case, his spouse was a devout Catholic and was concerned that the idea would take his attention away from their struggling teenager. This, in fact, did happen and thus reveals that this locution was a deception and not from God. The nature of the duties of our state in life can often be a powerful tool to help us discern God's will in these situations.

Test 8: A true locution will manifest words in such a way that they contain much deeper meaning than the words might otherwise hold if constructed by the imagination. Said another way, if a person were to communicate the same truth of this locution in speech, it would be difficult to construct rapidly in the same manner with respect to the depth, breadth, and impact of the locution itself. The locution has such an instantaneous deep gravity and resonance of meaning that it could not have been constructed instantly through human speech or through the imagination or the memory and could not have come from the enemy.

Test 9: Determine whether the locution causes confusion. The state of being bewildered or unclear in one's mind about something, or experiencing a lack of understanding or uncertainty as the result of a locution, is a bad sign. Confusion is never of God and thus is a definite sign of the inauthentic nature of the locution. As 1 Corinthians 14:33 reveals, "God is not a God of confusion but of peace."

Test 10: Discern whether the effects or fruits of the locution result in pride and self-satisfaction or in humility. If a locution inflames any vice in the soul, it should be rejected immediately. Authentic locutions will result in weakening unhealthy or disordered self-esteem and increasing humility — the soul will better remember its own sins and be forgetful of self-interest after receiving an authentic locution.

Test 11: In this test, St. Teresa details the way to discern what she calls the "devil's locutions." If the locution involves some action to be taken or some situation that requires anything to do with a third party, the locution should not be acted upon and should be discussed with a spiritual director to discern its authenticity. St. Teresa affirms that if it is authentic, the Lord will reveal this to the spiritual director. If the Lord does not give this confidence to the spiritual director, the soul has no obligation to follow through and should strive to put the locution out of its mind. In fact, St. Teresa is so adamant on this point that she warns, "I consider it very dangerous for a person to do anything but what he has been told to do and to follow his own opinion in this matter; so, I admonish you … in Our Lord's name, never to act thus."

As Teresa concludes her thoughts on locutions and ways to discern their authenticity, she notes that the devil "can do little or no harm if the soul is humble." Humility is the greatest antidote to demonic deception. In spite of the enemy's subtle working in this mansion and the very real possibility of the soul's being led astray by false locutions, the soul should feel some security here, not in itself, but in God's deep love for it and the assurance of His help and protection so long as it consistently strives for deeper self-knowledge of its weaknesses and its total dependence on God for everything. St. Teresa writes most beautifully and consolingly of the place of the soul in the hand of God in this mansion:

> It seems that Our Lord wants everyone to realize that such a person's soul is now His and that no one must touch it. People are welcome to attack her body, her honor, and her possessions, for any of these attacks will be to His Majesty's honor. But her soul they may not attack, for unless, with most blameworthy presumption, it tears itself away from its Spouse, He will protect it from the whole world, and indeed from all hell.

There is yet another phenomenon the soul in this or adjacent mansions may experience. Teresa describes this as a kind of sublime and transformative rapture that draws the soul to God in such a way that it is clearly not of the devil, since "such an experience could not possibly proceed from the imagination, and the devil could never reveal things which produce such results in the soul and leave it with such peace and tranquility and with so many benefits."[40] In reflecting on the outcomes, she provides four ways the soul can know, at this stage, whether this, or any related kind of spiritual experience, is authentically from God:

1. *Knowledge of the greatness of God:* The more the soul experiences an authentic encounter with God, the more it is deeply conscious of and in awe of the greatness of God.

2. *Self-knowledge and humility:* These virtues increase through "realizing how a thing like the soul, so base by comparison with One Who is the Creator of such greatness, has dared to offend Him and dares to raise its eyes to Him." Humility draws the soul to God and God to the soul.

3. *Supreme contempt for earthly things:* This contempt is a proper ordering of priorities that would remove earthly matters from any list of concern, "save those which can be employed in the service of so great a God."

4. *The encounter is unforgettable:* "These meetings with the Spouse remain so deeply engraved in the memory that I think it is impossible for the soul to forget them until it is enjoying them forever; if it did so, it would suffer the greatest harm. But the Spouse Who gives them to the soul has power also to give it grace not to lose them."[41]

St. Teresa further reflects that

God gives these souls the keenest desire not to displease Him in any respect whatsoever, however trivial, or to

---

[40] *Interior Castle*, Sixth Mansions, chap. 5.
[41] *Interior Castle*, Sixth Mansions, chap. 5.

commit so much as an imperfection if they can avoid doing so. For this reason alone, if for no other, the soul would like to flee from other people, and greatly envies those who lived, or have lived, in deserts. On the other hand, it would like to plunge right into the heart of the world, to see if by doing this it could help one soul to praise God more.[42]

St. Teresa emphasizes that the godly desires inspired by these experiences are "not fleeting but permanent."[43] Said another way, these experiences must be judged over a considerable period in order to reveal the permanence of their impact. They can rarely, in the moment, be accepted as authentic until the test of time reveals the true source.

St. Teresa further reveals the holy desires created in the soul through these sublime encounters with God; the deep desire to leave this life in order to be permanently with God, or to "see" Him face-to-face, burns within the soul. The only time this permanence temporarily seems to fade is when the Lord allows the soul to drift into desolation so that it will better realize that these gifts come from God alone and that nothing in the soul is capable of producing them. In this sense, it is possible that the devil may again be used as an instrument of God to aid the soul in that God may allow the enemy to tempt the soul to believe it is so spiritually mature that such gifts emerge primarily out of its own holiness, as if it produces them by its own power and virtue. Through the desolation the soul experiences, it will learn again and more deeply the remedy for such deception: that it can never,

---

[42] *Interior Castle*, Sixth Mansions, chap. 6.
[43] *Interior Castle*, Sixth Mansions, chap. 6.

by its own abilities, produce these spiritual experiences or the resulting profound quietness and peace that follow them, and thus it will be humbled before God and ever more grateful for the favors He bestows on it when it has done nothing to deserve them. Understanding what the Lord is doing in the moment of desolation further solidifies in the soul that the Lord is the One at work and it is He alone giving these extraordinary gifts, so that the soul does not appropriate them and fall into the sin of prideful usurpation.

St. Teresa spends time in this mansion detailing an aspect of spiritual warfare that, although it can reveal itself at any point in the spiritual life, seems more likely to arise in these latter stages. This aspect is that the soul is prone to be easily moved to an excessive experience of tears. St. Teresa notes that "it seems as if [those souls] will never make an end of weeping; having come to believe that tears are good, they make no attempt to control them." She then notes that the devil does his best in these cases to weaken the soul so that, as it is immersed in its tears, it is thereby "unable to practice prayer or to keep [the] Rule."[44] In general, a good test here is that if anything "good" tends to keep the soul from its commitments to daily mental prayer or other foundational spiritual exercises, or otherwise impedes its ability to fulfill with exacting attention the duties of its state in life, then those apparent "good" things have been twisted or come to be disordered in the life of the soul or else are an apparent good that the enemy has proposed to it in an effort to draw it away from what should be its focus. If the tears are truly a gift from God, they will produce comfort and tranquility along with humility. If these elements are not present, Teresa says it will do

---

[44] *Interior Castle*, Sixth Mansions, chap. 6.

no harm for the soul to remain suspicious and to test the spirits. And the soul should note again, as has been stated previously, Teresa's repeated insistence on the necessity of learning this mode of discernment in order to navigate these later mansions. At the most fundamental level, the good spirits will always lead the soul toward the truth of Scripture, the Magisterium of the Church, the sacraments, and the virtues of faith, hope, and love. The bad spirits will always lead the soul in the opposite direction, toward doubt, despair, and narcissism.[45]

The manifestation of tears can be challenging because they can arise from any number of factors, such as a lack of emotional sobriety, and they can even arise from the soul's own willfulness or pride. Tears and any other spiritual experience that may have a physical manifestation are worth examining in greater detail, and Teresa does branch out here into profound wisdom regarding the general disposition of the soul with respect to spiritual gifts. Following is a summary of her admonitions regarding the gift of tears; it also applies to the other gifts gratuitously given by God, most popularly known as the charismatic gifts (e.g., tongues and prophecy):

- Weeping (or any other spiritual gift) is far less efficacious than the exercise of the will in self-giving and self-denial and the practice of virtue. This is a good universal rule that will never harm the soul as it cautiously evaluates and interprets these experiences. This doesn't mean the soul should be fearful or resistant to the movements of the spirit that may affect its person, but simply that the

---

[45] To learn more, I recommend studying and faithfully practicing the disciplines found in my book *Spiritual Warfare and the Discernment of Spirits*.

soul always takes a stance of sobriety when it assesses the fruit and thus the source of any spiritual experience.

• The soul should be open to the gifts when they come but shouldn't seek to induce them through human means. This means that gratuitous gifts cannot be manufactured or taught. It warrants repeating because of the confusion of our times: a gift is given freely by God; it cannot be manufactured or taught. Teresa's thinking here is very much in line with the New Testament, where we read that there were only two preexisting conditions in those receiving charismatic gifts: (1) the soul desired God, and (2) those who had the gifts or the authority laid hands upon desirous souls and prayed for them. All other activities that seek to teach or elicit gifts are what St. Teresa would call human manipulation, and this leads to problematic outcomes, such as demonic deception or bodily or mental fatigue. She says, "The devil does his best, in such cases, to weaken them, so that they may be unable either to practice prayer or to keep their Rule."[46] As such, the fruits almost always reveal the roots or the source of the experience.

St. Teresa instructs the soul to allow the Lord to move in however and whenever He desires. Rather than chasing after an experience, which, in our day, can often manifest itself in an incessant quest for the latest conference or new manifestations of the "spirit," she admonishes the soul to focus on the practice of mental prayer by placing itself in the Lord's presence, meditating on His mercy and its lowliness, and accepting whatever comes from His hand, whether it be a rich sensory experience or a dry desert. In all

[46] *Interior Castle*, Sixth Mansions, chap. 6.

of this, if it walks in this way, the soul will have authentic peace and the enemy will have "less opportunity to fool" it.[47]

Another point St. Teresa addresses in the sixth mansion deals with a potential deception that applies to those in the latter stages of spiritual growth. This would, of course, include those navigating this mansion but also likely anyone in the late purgative through the illuminative way and beyond. The reason for this is that those in the illuminative way and beyond enter into a simpler kind of prayer — contemplative prayer — that is dominated by God's direct work in the soul, in contrast to the soul's work and effort. This kind of prayer no longer requires discursive meditation common to the purgative stage, and when the soul reaches the place of contemplative prayer, its ability to practice active meditation is frustrated to the point of needing to yield to the new kind of prayer that God is seeking to bring it to.

St. Teresa's contention here is that even if the soul experiences this simpler, contemplative prayer, it should never fail to give time for its heart and mind to ponder on the suffering of Jesus. She notes that some have tried to convince her that there is a point at which one progresses to such a place wherein they no longer need or receive any benefit from meditating on the Passion of Jesus. Her assertion is that this is not only wrong, but, in fact, is an attempted deception of the enemy of souls.

The great mystical Doctor goes on to make a very forceful argument on the need to meditate on Jesus' suffering on the soul's behalf regardless of where it is in its spiritual maturation:

> The last thing we should do is to withdraw of set purpose from our greatest help and blessing, which is the most

---

[47] *Interior Castle*, Sixth Mansions, chap. 6.

sacred Humanity of Our Lord Jesus Christ. I cannot believe that people can really do this; it must be that they do not understand themselves and thus do harm to themselves and to others. At any rate, I can assure them that they will not enter these last two Mansions; for, if they lose their Guide, the good Jesus, they will be unable to find their way; they will do well if they are able to remain securely in the other Mansions. For the Lord Himself says that He is the Way; the Lord also says that He is light and that no one can come to the Father save by Him.[48]

Is she saying that the soul in the contemplative realm should always force itself to continue praying with the use of meditative approaches such as *lectio divina* in its time of daily prayer in order to focus on the humanity of Jesus? St. Teresa is not arguing for this approach and states as much with pointed clarity. Instead, she wants to encourage the soul constantly keep before its eye and heart Jesus' suffering on its behalf. The soul can do this by praying the Sorrowful Mysteries slowly, by spiritual reading on the Passion or on the Sacred Heart, by making special meditations, such as the Stations of the Cross and so forth. These need not disrupt the normal daily mental prayer routine in order to bear fruit, as St. Teresa explains:

By meditation I mean prolonged reasoning with the understanding, in this way. We begin by thinking of the favor which God bestowed upon us by giving us His only Son; and we do not stop there but proceed to consider the mysteries of His whole glorious life. Or we begin with the

[48] *Interior Castle*, Sixth Mansions, chap. 7.

prayer in the Garden and go on rehearsing the events that follow until we come to the Crucifixion. Or we take one episode of the Passion—Christ's arrest, let us say—and go over this mystery in our mind, meditating in detail upon the points in it which we need to think over and to try to realize, such as the treason of Judas, the flight of the Apostles, and so on. This is an admirable and a most meritorious kind of prayer.[49]

In keeping with St. Teresa's advice, it is said of St. Thomas More that on Fridays he often spent the entire day in meditation on Jesus' suffering on our behalf. This seems to be a good practice and follows the tradition of fasting on Fridays in remembrance of Jesus' suffering. Certainly, it seems, this ongoing attentiveness to meditating on the Passion of Christ had a profound impact on St. Thomas's commitment to Christ and deepened his desire to serve the Lord with his whole heart, mind, soul, and strength such that he became a martyr for his Faith. The Church agrees with this sentiment, as every Friday the Liturgy of the Hours draws the faithful to those psalms that reveal the prayers and suffering of Jesus on the Cross.

Before leaving the sixth mansion, St. Teresa takes the soul on a tour of deceptions regarding intellectual visions that can afflict souls in this mansion. These are "visions" that are not in any way either physically or imaginatively visual, as the nomenclature might seem to indicate. Instead, these visions have to do with a certainty that Jesus is near to the soul. The primary signs that these visions are authentic are the same as those that are repeated often in St. Teresa's writings:

[49] *Interior Castle*, Sixth Mansions, chap. 7.

- The soul is at peace.
- The desire for God and to give oneself to God is increased.
- Humility increases in the soul.
- Sensitivity to any kind of sin or imperfection increases such that the soul is ever more deeply grieved at any possible or actual offense given to God.

St. Teresa asserts that when these factors are clearly manifest in the soul, the enemy cannot be the source of the vision, as he would be "furious" at seeing so much progress in the soul in this way.[50]

St. Teresa also reveals a phenomenon some souls might experience called an "imaginative vision." This kind of vision cannot be produced through normal practices of meditation, wherein the soul works to develop an understanding of God by, for instance, using its imagination to place itself in a scene in the Gospels. Instead, these visions come as a sudden surprise, complete and instantaneously, like a bolt of lightning. And like a bolt of lightning, their power and glory produce a kind of awe and fear that make a deep and lasting impression on the soul. As such, the enemy cannot produce this kind of vision. A deceptive attempt by the enemy to mimic this type of vision is often preceded by the desire of the soul to see such a vision, a desire that itself should be a caution to the attentive soul, since any seeking of that sort immediately signals a departure away from the seeking of God and His will alone and shifts instead toward the self and seeking some gift or manifestation of God. St. Teresa notes that this desire is an open door to deception. She muses that the enemy's attempts yield a kind of step-by-step building or progressive creation of the image of the vision, rather

---

[50] *Interior Castle*, Sixth Mansions, chap. 8.

than the image's appearing in a glorious flash of brilliance—a dynamic and living presence that is overwhelming and yields much knowledge to the soul about God. (You might remember a similar tactic employed by the demons with false locutions.) St. Teresa admonishes that the soul should never desire these kinds of phenomena but should only accept them as the Lord desires to give them or not. Similarly, as with all movements of God in the soul, these authentic visions result in:

- humility
- a sense of unworthiness in the soul to receive such gifts from God
- lasting fruits of holiness through growth in virtue
- peace
- deep certainty about the authenticity of the vision

This type of vision can also leave the soul in ecstasy for some time. Even though certainty about authenticity is always present when these visions come, St. Teresa warns that the soul should combat possible deception by sharing them with its spiritual director or another experienced person. This is sound advice when it comes to any type of perceived supernatural experience.

Finally, Teresa reveals the potential in these mansions of new kinds of visions, but she is not as clear about their nature as in previous descriptions of other spiritual experiences the soul may encounter here. She notes that these other kinds of visions cannot be from the enemy because, in a very sudden and complete way, they communicate sublime truths about God that draw the soul to God. The soul can use the previously enunciated tests to ensure that they are, in fact, from God. St. Teresa also offers perennial wisdom about the workings of the enemy that are valuable to emphasize here to remind the soul of their importance. She notes that the enemy is always "delighted to see a soul distressed or uneasy, because he knows that this will hinder it from employing itself in loving and praising God."[51] As such, the soul should never allow a lack of peace to remain present. Instead, it should fight against such afflictions of mind and spirit, knowing that they provide fertile ground for the enemy to plant his seeds of destruction.

Summary of the Battles of the Sixth Mansion

Demonic goal: To distort or mimic supernatural encounters in order to lead you to pride or distract you away from the primary duties of your state in life through demonically simulated or manipulated experiences.

Key tactics of the enemy

- To attempt to mimic the movements of God through seemingly authentic spiritual experiences
- To distort authentic spiritual experiences
- To deceive you into thinking that you are, in some way, the cause of spiritual experiences and thus lead you to pride and self-deception

How to battle these tactics successfully

The foundations previously laid for the fundamental disciplines of the soul on the path to God continue to be necessary throughout the soul's journey to help it deal with old and new challenges it faces on the path to these innermost rooms of the castle and thus deeper union with God. A few unique dispositions can also help in this realm:

- Be open to the movements of God but always hesitant to trust your own judgment of them.

---

[51] *Interior Castle*, Sixth Mansions, chap. 10.

- Submit these experiences to a spiritual director who is objectively able to help you understand their origins and implications.
- Never cling to any experience but, instead, hold them loosely and rest in the reality that you have all you need for your salvation in and through the normative means of the sacraments and authentic discipleship.

Spiritual encouragement: Those in this realm deal with much more subtle attempts at demonic manipulation that can be detected and overcome through persistent study, application of Teresa's tests for discerning the authenticity of spiritual experiences, spiritual direction with a learned and experienced director, and the foundational disciplines of authentic discipleship.

Questions for Reflection

What are the primary ways in which the enemy can deceive you at this stage of your spiritual growth?

Have you ever experienced something that sounds like St. Teresa's description of a locution or any other supernatural experience?

- *If you believe it was authentic, how have you tested it and found it to be so?*

- *If you believe it was inauthentic, how have you tested it and found it to be a deception?*

- *Have you ever fallen into the trap of trusting your own interpretation without any guidance from a spiritual director?*

- *What would you do differently if you had to face the same situation again?*

Why is it so important to have a spiritual director to help you discern what seem to be supernatural communications?

How does St. Teresa help you to understand your relationship with charismatic gifts?

What does St. Teresa advise you to focus on instead of seeking spiritual experiences?

Have you ever experienced what you think might be a vision? How does St. Teresa advise these visions be tested?

What are the general signs or fruits of authentic spiritual experiences? How do these relate to your life?

What does St. Teresa reveal is the most powerful antidote to demonic deception? How can you deepen the potency of this antidote at this stage of your spiritual life?

7

The Battles of the Seventh Mansion

The last stop in the soul's journey to God is a glorious and encouraging one. St. Teresa notes that there is not much spiritual warfare in this seventh and last mansion:

> The difference between this Mansion and the rest has already been explained. There are hardly any of the periods of aridity or interior disturbance in it which at one time or another have occurred in all the rest, but the soul is almost always in tranquility. It is not afraid that this sublime favor may be counterfeited by the devil but retains the unwavering certainty that it comes from God. For, as has been said, the senses and faculties have no part in this: His Majesty has revealed Himself to the soul and taken it with Him into a place where, as I believe, the devil will not enter, because the Lord will not allow him to do so; and all the favors which the Lord grants the soul here, as I have said, come quite independently of the acts of the soul itself, apart from that of its having committed itself wholly to God.[52]

---

[52] *Interior Castle*, Seventh Mansions, chap. 3.

Indeed, in closing, there is not much to be said about this final mansion with respect to spiritual warfare. The soul who reaches this mansion has found its way through the castle by cooperating with God's grace and experiences the Lord Himself; it needs no further guidance, nor does it need a description of what the experience of this union will be like, for the Lord will give the soul who meets Him here the desires of its heart in such a way that defies description. This is not to say that the soul doesn't need constant spiritual direction, care, and formation. The soul must always work to retain spiritual disciplines and to guard against the flesh's rising up to rule the spirit again.

The soul who has yet to know these heights should long for this intimate encounter with the Lord as the entire goal of its earthly life and hold the experience of it, once received safely in the deepest recesses of its heart, as the singular and sublime treasure of the foretaste of Heaven that it is.

It is a joy for the healthy and mature soul to look forward to a decreasing intensity of the demonic trials, but it is an even greater joy to know that there is a time when these completely or almost completely dissipate. It is vital to note at this point that every soul is called to this level or depth of contemplation and union with God. Even more glorious is that the Lord gives to every soul in Baptism, in a latent sense, the grace to know this great union and also gives actual grace to bring about that to which He calls the soul. Not all souls reach the seventh mansion, but all are absolutely called into this deep place of love and healing where the enemy's power to deceive and harm is greatly, if not wholly, diminished. The soul who does not labor with single-minded purpose to eventually dwell here is responsible for that, as can be seen by all Teresa has shared about what is required of the soul. God never fails to provide all help and grace to the soul to ensure that it *can* attain this height of union *if it chooses to do so and is willing to persevere* and fight for this, the "pearl of great price" (see Matt. 13:46), and choose God before all.

So too, in the tradition of the great saints of the Church who, like Teresa herself, have left behind them the story of their own journeys to God so that future souls might follow the model of this "great cloud of witnesses" (see Heb. 12:1) who have gone before, the soul in this mansion can look back over the battle-ground it has conquered with God's help and see how mighty the Lord is and how "all things work together for the good to those who love God" (see Rom. 8:28). From the vantage point of these dwelling places, the soul who has found its way to union with God can see clearly how little power the demons truly have over the soul who knows to whom it belongs, is rooted in prayer, knows well how to discern the workings of the enemy, and has been invested with all the necessary virtues in Christ. The soul sees, in fact, how the devil's evil efforts have borne fruit in the soul through testing and purification, like silver and gold in the refiners fire (see Zech. 13:9), and have helped to propel it toward eternity. For God uses the devil as His own instrument in the sanctification of souls, a paradoxical mode of resistance training, to raise up valiant lover-soldiers who will fight for and worship their Lord and King in the holy and sacred heart of the castle.

What Next?

A significant challenge emerges when we read the writings of great saints such as Teresa of Avila or John of the Cross. What is often difficult for the average reader is to understand the context and assumptions of the writer. The wise reader might ask, "What was left unsaid that is important for me to understand about the fullness of this journey to God?" This book has focused on exploring St. Teresa's wisdom and perspective on spiritual warfare as it relates to prayer and the soul's growth toward union with God. But now what? What steps can the soul take next in light of this new, exciting, but perhaps also overwhelming, awareness of these truths of the spiritual life? How can the soul really put this wisdom to work in its own life?

What follows are several recommendations for the soul who is truly motivated to put in the effort necessary to experience the profound spiritual breakthroughs and to progress more surely along the path St. Teresa has outlined in *The Interior Castle*:

1. Read St. Teresa of Avila's autobiography, slowly and meditatively, over the next year. Set aside a specific time each day to place yourself under the gaze of

Christ, open with prayer asking for His help and His grace, and then read the story of her life for ten to fifteen minutes. Once you have completed her auto-biography, read *The Interior Castle* in the same way. St. Teresa's autobiography is in no way a boring reflection on her life. Instead, it is a fascinating exploration of the heart and life of a saint that provides powerful insights into what it means to be an authentic disciple of Jesus and shows the path Teresa illustrates in *The Interior Castle* as it plays out in a single human life.

2. At the same time, if you have not already done so, begin the practice of daily mental prayer as described in the free course on mental prayer available at Apos-toliViae.org (see "Spiritual Reading and Online Re-sources" for this and other courses mentioned below). Even if you have some experience with daily mental prayer, I strongly recommend that you take this course.

3. Begin to make a daily examen to assess your move-ments toward or away from God during the day and consider tracking in a journal your progress and goals for growth in virtue. This will be a valuable tool to bring with you to meetings with your spiritual director and can assist you in preparing your plan of love and in making solid confessions.

4. Begin frequenting the sacraments of the Eucharist and Penance more often. The best practice for the sacrament of Penance is to go at least once a month. Souls truly intent on traversing the hard terrain to the center of the castle should receive the Eucharist as often as possible; strive for more than just the Sunday obligation as your circumstances and state of life allow.

5. Read about the Paradigm of Ascent below and take
the free course on this topic at ApostoliViae.org.

These foundational practices and formation will provide you
with a rich experience and spiritual growth that will allow you to
understand St. Teresa when you return to enter *The Interior Castle*
in its more complete expression. In fact, if you do as I suggest, by
the time you get to reading *The Interior Castle*, you will already
be inside the castle (if you were not already) and thus far better
able to understand the lay of the land and what is happening to
you there than those who approach it unprepared.

St. Teresa never intended for *The Interior Castle* to be read
by those who could not understand it because they were not yet
practicing foundational spiritual disciplines. Yes, her work is
open for all to understand, but it cannot be understood by those
who simply read the book as an intellectual exercise rather than
using it as a guide for the journey that she assumes the reader is
already making!

The Paradigm of Ascent as a Pathway Forward

To help you better understand the dynamics of that journey, I
provide below a brief summary of what I call the Paradigm of
Ascent.™ [53] This framework represents the foundational practices
of every saint of the past and of every holy person alive today.
These are practices that St. Teresa assumed would be in place in
the life of every reader who attempted to understand and follow
what she outlines in *The Interior Castle*. The truths revealed in

---

[53] Note that this trademark is to ensure its proper use. It is a
very simple but powerful model that can easily be trivialized
by those who use it without sufficient formation behind each
of its components.

the paradigm are foundational in that, if they are not all present in some substantive way in your life, a deeper understanding of the interior life will remain beyond your grasp. This is a bad thing only if you fail to take the next steps to remedy whatever deficiency you uncover.

The first foundational truth is that you must have an authentic yes in your heart to God to begin your journey into the castle. It is not enough merely to know about God or even to practice your Faith: you must know God intimately. This is the path of the mystics, but it is also the path every soul can know and must embrace to get to Heaven. This path is often obscure to most Catholics because it is not common for someone already in the Church to hear a pronounced or dramatic call to conversion. This call to conversion and even the warnings of Hell, however, were offered frequently by Jesus to those who were among His closest followers. Though you have been baptized and confirmed, you still must constantly recognize your need for God and for the conversion of life that draws you ever closer to Him.

The second foundational element is the most important support for your yes of the heart, and it consists of the Sacraments of the Eucharist and regular Confession. You should participate in the Holy Sacrifice of the Mass not only on Sundays (because it is a mortal sin to miss Mass on Sunday without good reason) but as frequently as possible, because the Eucharist is the most powerful sustenance of your faith. The Sacrament of Penance and Reconciliation is also necessary to support your yes. Too often, Catholics underestimate the power of this sacrament. You might think of it merely as a remedy for sin, which is true, but it is also a great grace to strengthen you against falling into sin again. Said another way, the Sacrament of Penance both provides forgiveness of sins and strengthens you in your efforts to fight sin. It is also the most significant weapon against Satan in spiritual warfare in the Church's arsenal. Regardless, if you are not reconciled to God and not living in a state of grace, you are cut off from the life of grace and will not be able to discern properly the difference between the inspirations and influence of God and the temptations and false lies of the devil. If you are not in a state of grace, you have fundamentally said no to God and His plan for your life and yes to the devil.

Because of the rampant poor catechesis of our time, I must be absolutely clear on this point. Living in a state of grace means that you are living without having unconfessed mortal sins and you are following the teachings of the Church in every aspect of your life. The *Catechism of the Catholic Church* is very clear on these matters and should be studied by every serious Catholic. The diagram below reveals the beginning elements of your foundation in the paradigm to ascend to greater holiness and their relationship with one another.

The third foundational element to authentic discipleship is daily prayer. The most powerful daily prayers are mental prayer and the Rosary. Sts. Teresa of Avila and Alphonsus Liguori, both Doctors of the Church, consider daily mental prayer to be necessary for salvation because of the impact on the soul of those who daily draw near to their Savior in dedicated intimacy. A sound and very practical understanding of the practice of daily mental prayer can be found in my book *Into the Deep: Finding Peace through Prayer*. The Rosary, as revealed by our Blessed Mother, is necessary both for your salvation and that of the world. Together, these two daily prayers provide protection as a kind of shield and nurtures your yes, which allows you to move forward in faith.[54] With these daily practices in place, our diagram now looks like this and begs for a final aspect necessary for balance.

The fourth foundational element to your discernment is *ascesis*. This ancient Greek word simply means "exercise." In our usage, that exercise is to exert conscious daily and deliberate effort away from sin and selfishness and toward self-giving to God and your neighbor. It is the practical result of what Jesus meant when He said, "If any man would come after me, let him deny himself and take up his cross and follow me" (Matt. 16:24). Ascesis is self-giving and self-denial—saying no to the draws of your lower nature in order to say yes to giving yourself completely to God and to those whom He has placed in your care or in your

---

[54] Whether you have yet to take up the practice of the Rosary or are a long-time practitioner and need to go deeper or break the pattern of rote familiarity, you will find helpful *The Contemplative Rosary*, which I co-authored with Connie Rossini.

circle of influence. Ascesis is simply what it means to truly follow Jesus. The funny thing is that if you pursue the sacraments and prayer the way the saints did, your practice of ascesis is already well under way!

This final element completes what I like to call a "saint-making machine." These basic elements are in place in the life of every saint and everyone who makes progress in the spiritual life toward God and peace and away from sin and the sorrows of sin. This Paradigm of Ascent™ is also the necessary basis for beginning to distinguish between the voice and influence of God and the voice and influence of the enemy of your soul.

As you begin to implement these practices, you will, by God's grace and provision, lay a foundation that is, in and of itself, the most powerful healing and liberating force you can know. You will begin living by what is known in Catholic Tradition as a rule of life, or what we call in our community of Apostoli Viae a "plan of love." A plan of love is simply a purposeful way to live and love God and those He has placed in our care. A good plan always has concrete commitments that you make to God and your loved ones on a daily, weekly, or monthly basis. A simple plan of love might look something like this:

• Daily mental prayer: wake up at 6:00 a.m. and pray for ten minutes, focusing on that day's Gospel reading for Mass.
• Daily Rosary: pray one decade on the way to work.
• Attend Mass every Sunday without fail.
• Go to Confession every other week.

The final step in your foundation is what is known as the examen, or examination of conscience. You might have heard the phrase in business "What gets measured gets done." The same principle applies in the life of the soul who truly desires to give itself to God and to know the peace and joy He has for it. It is common to hear folks shy away from the examen because they have been taught a predominantly negative approach that is solely focused on where they have failed or what they have done wrong. This is not the approach that I recommend. Instead, I encourage practicing the examen in a way that is focused on God's redemptive power and mercy, not on your weaknesses and failures. As St. Paul recalled, "He said to me, 'My grace is sufficient for you, for my power is made perfect in weakness.' ... For when I am weak, then I am strong" (2 Cor. 12:9–10).

The approach I recommend looks something like this: Every night before going to bed, take five minutes to review your day. Ask the Lord and the Blessed Mother to reveal what you need to know. Then step into your "mental helicopter," fly up about twenty feet and then fly back to when you got out of bed in the morning. Then slowly fly over your day from morning to evening, asking two simple questions:

1. *What have I been able to do, by the grace of God, that honors Him and others?* When you discover these things, express praise and thanksgiving to God. This can be as simple as "Thank You, Lord, for the ability to pray

according to my plan of love when I didn't feel like doing so."

2. *How have I failed to honor God and others?* When you discover these things, continue to pray in thanksgiving, something like this: "Thank You, Lord, for revealing my sin to me so that I can be forgiven and strengthened to overcome this sin in the future. Thank You for Your promise and provision of forgiveness and strength against sin and temptation."

Now, this may seem very simple—and it is. However, don't be fooled. This powerful practice is no less important than a compass to someone seeking to find his way through the wilderness. It keeps you awake to your progress on the narrow way to Heaven, and it helps ensure that you stay on the path. It also perfects your trust in God and deepens your understanding of yourself as a beloved child, wholly dependent on His help and mercy for every good in your life. As you have seen in traveling through the castle with St. Teresa, staying awake is critical to hearing and heeding the voice of God and avoiding the influence of the enemy of your soul.

Conclusion

My motivation in writing this book was to awaken or reawaken you to, or to reinforce, the reality of the challenges you will face and can overcome (by the grace of God) as you progress toward God, who awaits you in the heart of the castle. My aim was also to instill a deeper awareness of the spiritual reality and the demonic entities around you that seek to hinder your progress, along with the remedies that the Lord has provided to assist you along your way. Not many laypeople have the grave privilege of being involved in exorcisms or the liberation of souls from demonic bondage. My experiences in exorcisms and deliverance ministry have been formative and have given me a greater awareness of what is real and what is illusory. I believe this greater awareness is vital for our time because the darkness is settling in at a rate that I have not seen in my lifetime. I once considered the practice of discernment of spirits as revealed by St. Ignatius of Loyola and St. John of the Cross to be a good thing, but not necessary for all believers. Now I consider the disciplined practice of Ignatian discernment of spirits and the lived perspective of the Carmelite Doctors on how they aid the soul along the way to God to be vital to the survival of the Faith in souls who are unprepared or ill-prepared for what is now and what is to come. To discover all you need to learn to fight well, overcome the tactics of the enemy, and help others to do so, see the Resources for Continued Spiritual Growth.

May Jesus Christ be praised now and forever!

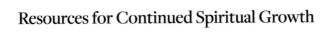

Resources for Continued Spiritual Growth

Spiritual Reading and Online Resources

If you are ready to engage more deeply in the battle for peace and strength in the storm and deepen your relationship with the God who longs for you, go to ApostoliViae.org and create a free profile. Once you complete that process, go to the Courses page to find a series of free mini courses on overcoming habitual sin, discernment of spirits, mental prayer, the examen, and much more. As well, you will gain access to a printable summary guide for both the examen and the rules of discernment that will reinforce what you have read in this book and help you to learn and apply the powerful life-changing wisdom of St. Teresa of Avila.

Here are additional recommended resources to help you on your journey.

Spiritual Warfare

Spiritual Warfare and the Discernment of Spirits by Dan Burke gives a foundational understanding of the battleground of the mind, how the enemy works in this area, and how Scripture and the wisdom of St. Ignatius of Loyola can help you fight back against the world, the flesh, and the devil and win (SpiritualDirection. com/shop).

Discernment of Spirits in Marriage by Fr. Timothy Gallagher offers a very practical and powerful way to protect, fight, and win against the forces that divide faithful marriages (SpiritualDirection.com/shop).

Spiritual Warfare and the Family by Kathleen Beckman provides an in-depth look at the cultural and spiritual forces working against the family and how families can deal effectively with these challenges. It includes a treasury of prayers for the laity to use in spiritual warfare (SpiritualDirection.com/shop).

Deliverance Prayers for Use by the Laity by Fr. Chad Ripperger is a collection of prayers from the public domain and from the Church's treasury for waging spiritual warfare (ApostoliViae. org/shop).

Daily Spiritual Sustenance

SpiritualDirection.com is meant to help you to grow spiritually by providing thousands of articles, videos, and other powerful materials rooted in the Magisterium and the faithful mystical tradition of the Church. Be sure to sign up for the e-mail digest, which will provide you with new insights on the journey every week.

Targeted Formation in the Spiritual Life and Spiritual Theology

Avila Institute for Spiritual Formation (Avila-Institute.org). The Avila Institute provides spiritual formation to laity, priests, and religious worldwide through live online classes. There are studies at a level for busy people as well as graduate studies for those who have the time and inclination.

Additional Spiritual Reading

PRAYER

Into the Deep: Finding Peace Through Prayer by Dan Burke is the simplest, most straightforward book in print on how to begin or deepen your prayer life (SpiritualDirection.com/shop).

Finding God through Meditation by St. Peter of Alcantara, and updated and introduced by Dan Burke, helps those who have practiced mental prayer daily for some time to dive deeper into prayer and devotion. St. Peter was a spiritual director to the great mystic St. Teresa of Avila (SpiritualDirection.com/shop).

PEACE — FINDING, ACQUIRING, AND
UNDERSTANDING THE MOVEMENTS OF GOD IN PEACE

Searching for and Maintaining Peace by Fr. Jacques Philippe, a well-known spiritual writer and retreat master, explains how to grow in love of God and neighbor by acquiring and maintaining peace of heart.

Discernment of Spirits by Fr. Timothy Gallagher provides you with a deeper insight into discernment of spirits and is a good follow-up to *Spiritual Warfare and the Discernment of Spirits* (ApostoliViae. org/shop).

RULE OF LIFE, ROOT SIN, AND OVERCOMING HABITUAL SIN

Navigating the Interior Life: Spiritual Direction and the Journey to God by Dan Burke provides an understanding of how to grow spiritually with or without a spiritual director (SpiritualDirection.com/shop).

The Seven Deadly Sins: A Thomistic Guide to Vanquishing Vice and Sin by Kevin Vost is a very accessible and practical treatment of understanding sin and how to overcome it (SpiritualDirection. com/shop).

Spiritual Combat by Lorenzo Scupoli provides wisdom on how to overcome sin and grow spiritually. St. Francis de Sales always carried this book and regularly promoted it (SpiritualDirection. com/shop).

SACRAMENTS

Confession: Its Fruitful Practice is a very brief but powerful guide to the fruitful practice of Confession (TANBooks.com).

The Catholic Mass: Steps to Restore the Centrality of God in the Liturgy by Bishop Athanasius Schneider with Aurelio Porfiri assists us in developing Godward humility by reemphasizing the homage we render God in the Mass (SophiaInstitute.com).

A Devotional Journey into the Mass: How Mass Can Become a Time of Grace, Nourishment, and Devotion by Christopher Carstens helps committed Catholics learn how to enter more deeply into the mysteries of the Holy Sacrifice of the Mass (SpiritualDirection.com/shop).

Daily Examen Guide

A daily examen enables you to stay awake and attentive to God's voice and His inner movements in your heart. Once awake, you can better understand who you and who where you are in relationship with God and His will for your life.

Simple Daily Redemptive Examen Guide

1. Set aside five minutes to reflect on your day, either in the evening or the next morning.
2. Ask the Lord to help you see what He wants you to see.
3. Ask the Blessed Mother to help you see what the Lord wants you to see.
4. Sit quietly for a moment. Then, in your imagination, get into a helicopter and fly back and hover over the beginning of your day. Now slowly fly forward in time, observing in your day two things:
   • Areas where you sinned or fell short of your desire and God's desire for you.

- Areas where you succeeded, particularly with respect to where you have worked to improve your behavior in any way.

5. As you consider both of these areas, with respect to sin or shortcomings, first give thanks to God for revealing these areas that need to be healed, and then ask Him for forgiveness. Second, in areas where you have succeeded, give God thanks and praise for His grace and for giving you the ability to follow Him well and honor others well.

6. Close this time of prayer with thanksgiving for God's forgiveness. If you have committed mortal sin, get to Confession as soon as you can.

Confession Guide

❧∞❧

Five Steps for a Good Confession

1. Examine your conscience: recall the sins that you have committed since your last good confession.[55]
2. Be sincerely sorry for your sins. If you have trouble with this, take time to meditate on Jesus' suffering because of your sin. You might pray an act of contrition.

ACT OF CONTRITION

Lord Jesus Christ, true God and true man, my
Creator and Redeemer, I am heartily sorry for
having offended You, and I detest all my sins because
I dread the loss of Heaven and the pains of Hell, but
most of all because they offend You, my God, who
are all good and deserving of all my love. I firmly
resolve, with the help of Your grace, to confess my
sins, to do penance, to avoid whatever leads me to
sin, and to amend my life. Amen.

---

[55] See "Examination of Conscience before Confession" below.

3. Confess your sins to the priest. Make certain that you confess all your mortal sins and the number of times you committed them.
4. Resolve to amend your life.
5. After your confession, do the penance the priest assigned you.

Examination of Conscience before Confession
Areas to Consider

- Each area of my life should be considered: my family, my friends, my work, my prayer, those I work and live with, and so forth.
- How have I sinned in thought, word, and deed? Even if I did not gossip in word, did I judge someone in my thoughts?
- Have I committed any sins of omission? These may be more serious than sins of commission. Have I omitted to say my prayers? Have I omitted to be aware of and respond to the needs of family?

Examination of Conscience

You might examine your conscience in light of the Ten Commandments or the seven deadly sins.

THE TEN COMMANDMENTS
1. I, the Lord, am your God. You shall not have other gods besides me.
2. You shall not take the name of the Lord, your God, in vain.
3. Remember to keep holy the Lord's Day.

4. Honor your father and your mother.
5. You shall not kill.
6. You shall not commit adultery.
7. You shall not steal.
8. You shall not bear false witness against your neighbor.
9. You shall not covet your neighbor's wife.
10. You shall not covet your neighbor's goods.

The Seven Deadly Sins

The seven deadly sins are pride or narcissism, lust, anger, covetousness, envy, sloth, and gluttony.[56]

You can find examination-of-conscience guides based on the Ten Commandments online. Below are guiding questions to examine your conscience in light of the seven deadly sins.

Pride or Narcissism

Pride is the mother of all sin.[57] Vanity, an expression of pride, is excessive concern about what others think of me.[58] Pusillanimity, timidity, and cowardice are opposites of pride.

Have I refused to admit my own weaknesses?

Have I dwelt on the failings of others?

Have I judged others in my thoughts or words?

Have I ranked myself better than others?

---

[56] You can use the acronym PLACES-G to help you remember this list of sins.

[57] Read more about pride in St. Thomas Aquinas's *Summa Theologica* II-II, q. 162.

[58] Vanity, an expression of pride, is excessive concern about what others think of me. See St. Thomas Aquinas, *Summa Theologica*, II-II, q. 132.

The Devil in the Castle

Have I borne hatred or disdain for another?
Have I refused to learn from others?
Have I been irritable with others?
Have I been critical of others?
Have I been slow to listen to others and quick to speak
over them?
Have I been stubborn or refused to admit I was wrong?
Have I refused to accept that another person had a better
idea than mine?
Have I been arrogant?
Have I held others in contempt?
Have I reacted negatively when questioned?
Have I been overly concerned about what others think of
me? Have I allowed this to motivate my actions?
Have I failed to follow God's will out of fear of what others
might think of me?
Have I lied or exaggerated to make myself look good?
Have I wasted undue time and money on clothes and
appearance?
Have I been content with my lowly position, or have I
resented the role that Christ asks of me?
Do I constantly take selfies or spend time primping and
correcting my hair, clothing, or other aspects of my
appearance?
Have I neglected to use the talents that God has
given me?
Have I shied away from my duties or from doing or
saying what is right out of fear of how others will
respond?
Have I failed to give witness in public to my faith in
Christ?

LUST

Lust is disordered desire for sexual pleasure, isolated from its procreative and unitive purpose.[59]

> Have I maintained custody of my eyes, or have I allowed them to wander? "Every one who looks at a woman lustfully has already committed adultery with her in his heart" (Matt. 5:28).
> Have I viewed other people as mere sexual objects rather than as persons to be loved and served?
> Have I viewed pornography or related sexual or sexualized material on the Internet, on TV, or on social media?
> Have I engaged in romantic fiction leading to sexual fantasy?
> Have I entertained impure thoughts?
> Have I engaged in masturbation, alone or with another?

ANGER OR WRATH

Anger is undue desire for vengeance—undue in cause or in amount.[60] Impatience is also considered here.

> Have I harbored resentment, grudges, and hatred in my thoughts?
> Have I nurtured imaginary angry conversations?
> Have I been slow to forgive?
> Have I lost my temper?
> Have I carried my crosses without complaint or self-pity?
> Have I been impatient with people, family, events, sufferings, sicknesses?

---

[59] See St. Thomas Aquinas, *Summa Theologica* II-II, q. 153; *Catechism of the Catholic Church* (CCC), no. 2351.
[60] See St. Thomas Aquinas, *Summa Theologica*, II-II, q. 158.

The Devil in the Castle

AVARICE OR COVETOUSNESS

Avarice is the excessive love of possessing things.[61]

> Have I been overly concerned about my comfort and
> well-being?
> Have I been resentful of my lack of money or resources?
> Have I been generous in giving? Have I given with a
> cheerful heart?
> Have I avoided sacrificial giving? Do I give only what is
> easy to give?
> Have I cheated or stolen?
> Have I failed to pay my bills on time?
> Have I used people for my own ends and advantage?
> Have I wasted money on things I don't absolutely need?

ENVY AND JEALOUSY

Envy is sadness at the happiness of another.[62] Envy can lead to
gossip and judgmental thoughts.

> Have I envied or been jealous of the abilities, talents, ideas,
> good looks, intelligence, clothes, possessions, or money
> of anyone?
> Have I judged others in my thoughts?
> Have I damaged the reputation of another person by my
> words, attitude, or looks, reactions, or responses?
> Have I repeated accusations that might not be true? Have I
> exaggerated?
> Have I failed to defend the reputation of others?
> Have I failed to keep a secret?

---

[61] See St. Thomas Aquinas, *Summa Theologica*, II-II, q. 118.
[62] See St. Thomas Aquinas, *Summa Theologica*, II-II, q. 36.

Do I despise others of different races, classes, or cultures?
Have I lied, exaggerated, or distorted the truth?

SLOTH OR APATHY

Sloth is a kind of laziness, especially in the things of God. It is a sorrow in the face of spiritual good; it makes me lethargic and want to do nothing, or it drives me to neglect spiritual goods.[63] Punctuality and self-discipline are helpful in overcoming sloth.

Toward God

Have I sought God above all else, or have I put other
things (e.g., friendships, ambition, comfort, and ease)
ahead of Him?

Have I gotten so caught up in the things of this world that
I've forgotten God?

Have I risked losing my faith or piety by bad company, bad
reading, cowardice, or pride?

Have I trusted God, especially in times of difficulty?

Have I attended Mass every Sunday?

Have I neglected to say my daily prayers?

Have I entertained distractions in prayer or failed to
give God due concentration in prayer or during Mass?
(Note: Not giving God the effort He deserves in prayer
is a sin, but it is not the same thing as involuntary
weakness in mental distractions.)

Have I made a prayerful preparation before Mass and a
good thanksgiving after Mass?

Have I received Holy Communion while in a state of
serious sin?

[63] See St. Thomas Aquinas, *Summa Theologica*, II-II, q. 35.

The Devil in the Castle

After committing a mortal sin, have I neglected to go to
Confession before receiving Holy Communion?
Have I taken the Lord's name in vain or used other foul
language?

Toward my family
Have I been more focused on myself than on the needs
of my family?
Have I spent time with my family?
How have I manifested my concern for them?
Have I been forgiving and tolerant of them?
Have I scandalized them by a bad or lazy example?

Toward my neighbor
Have I been lazy in helping others?
Have I been attentive to the needs of my neighbor, espe-
cially my immediate or extended family members?
Has my conversation been focused on my own pleasure
or on others?
Has my humor been insensitive to others?

Punctuality and self-discipline
Have I wasted other people's time or dishonored them
by being late? Have I failed to keep my commitments
regarding being on time?
Have I sinned against God and the congregation by being
late for Mass through my own fault?
Have I gone to sleep on time?
Have I made good use of my time, or have I wasted it
(e.g., on my cell phone, watching TV, gaming, or on
the Internet)?

Have I planned good use of relaxation and recreation,
knowing that I need to rest well in order to serve well?

GLUTTONY

Gluttony is the inordinate or excessive desire for, focus on, attachment to, or use of food or other material goods.[64]

Have I consumed more than I need to — more than my
body needs to maintain a healthy weight?

Have I consumed food or drink that is damaging to my
body to satisfy my tastes or appetites?

Have I spent inordinate time engaging with food (or other
material things) or fantasizing about food (or other
material things)?

Have I spent excessive money on food?

Have I consumed alcohol excessively? Have I driven after
drinking?

Have I eaten greedily with little consideration for those at
table with me?

Have I failed to give money to help the hungry?

Have I failed to practice fasting and self-denial, especially
on Fridays?

Have I failed to abstain from meat on Fridays?

Have I always fasted an hour before receiving Holy
Communion at Mass?

Do I spend excessive energy and expense seeking to
ensure that my food or environment is perfectly to
my desires (temperature, texture, atmosphere)?

Do I spent excessive energy and expense seeking
comfort?

---

[64] See St. Thomas Aquinas, *Summa Theologica*, II-II, q. 148.

Glossary of Terms

Affective: See "Prayer—affective."

Appetites—disordered: Inordinate and willful desires for created things or circumstances not rightly ordered to moral or spiritual good that impede union with God and darken, defile, weaken, and torment the soul (author's definition).

Aridity: The state of a soul devoid of sensible consolation (see "Sensible consolation"), which makes it very difficult to pray. It may be caused by something physical, such as illness, or voluntary self-indulgence, or an act of God, who is leading a person through trial to contemplation.

Ascetical theology: The science of the saints based on a study of their lives. It is aimed to make people holy by explaining what sanctity is and how to attain it. It is the science of leading

Unless otherwise noted, these terms and definitions are taken from the *Modern Catholic Dictionary* by Fr. John A. Hardon, S.J., Real Presence Association, http://www.therealpresence. org/dictionary/adict.htm. Used with permission.

souls in the ways of Christian perfection through growth in charity and the practice of prayer leading to contemplation. It is that part of spiritual theology that concentrates on man's cooperation with grace and the need for human effort to grow in sanctity.

Asceticism: Spiritual effort or exercise in the pursuit of virtue. The purpose is to grow in Christian perfection. Its principles and norms are expanded in ascetical theology.

Attachment: An emotional dependence, either of one person on another, or of a person on some real or illusory object. Attachments play an important role in spiritual development, since the first condition for progress in sanctity is some mastery over one's inordinate attachments.

Charity: The infused supernatural virtue by which a person loves God above all things for his own sake and loves others for God's sake. It is a virtue based on divine faith or in belief in God's revealed truth and is not acquired by mere human effort. It can be conferred only by divine grace. Because it is infused along with sanctifying grace, it is frequently identified with the state of grace. Therefore, a person who has lost the supernatural virtue of charity has lost the state of grace, although he may still possess the virtues of hope and faith.

Concupiscence: Insubordination of man's desires to the dictates of reason, and the propensity of human nature to sin as a result of original sin. More commonly, it refers to the spontaneous movement of the sensitive appetites toward whatever the imagination portrays as pleasant and away from whatever it portrays as painful. However, concupiscence also includes the unruly desires of the will, such as pride, ambition, and envy.

Confession—devotional: The practice of regular Confession even when one is not aware of mortal or even venial sins. This practice includes setting and keeping a specific schedule of self-examination and Confession. This may also include the confession of past mortal or venial sins even if confessed previously in specific or in general. Devotional Confession can and should also make note of imperfections (see "Imperfections") though they are not sufficient matter for absolution. In such a case, previously confessed sins, especially related to one's predominant fault, should be mentioned. Author's note: Without the guidance of a spiritual director, this practice is not recommended for those who suffer with scrupulosity.

Consolation: An interior movement aroused in the soul, by which it is inflamed with love of its Creator and Lord. It is likewise consolation when one sheds tears that move to the love of God, whether it be because of sorrow for sins, or because of the sufferings of Christ our Lord, or for any other reason that is immediately directed to the praise and service of God. Consolation can also be every increase of faith, hope, and love, and all interior joy that invites and attracts to what is heavenly and to the salvation of one's soul by filling it with peace and quiet in its Creator and Lord (adapted from St. Ignatius of Loyola, *Spiritual Exercises* 316).

Contemplation: See "Prayer—contemplation—infused."

Detachment: In asceticism, the withholding of undue affection for creatures for the sake of the Creator. When mortal sin is involved, detachment is imperative for salvation. Detachment from creatures that are an obstacle to complete service of God is a normal condition for growth in holiness.

Discernment of spirits: The ability to distinguish whether a given idea or impulse in the soul comes from the good spirit or from the evil spirit. It may be an act of the virtue of prudence, or a special gift of supernatural grace, or both. In persons who are seriously intent on doing God's will, the good spirit is recognized by the peace of mind and readiness for sacrifice that a given thought or desire produces in the soul. The evil spirit produces disturbance of mind and a tendency to self-indulgence. An opposite effect is produced by both spirits toward sinners.

Disordered affections: See "Attachment."

Disposition: A quality or condition of a person necessary for the performance of some action. Commonly applied to the conditions required for the valid reception or administration of the sacraments, as the state of grace is required for the Sacrament of the Eucharist or sincere contrition to receive absolution in the Sacrament of Penance.

Doctor of the Church: A title given since the Middle Ages to certain saints whose writing or preaching is outstanding for guiding the faithful in all periods of the Church's history.

Dryness: See "Aridity."

Ecstasy: An infused state in which the soul is drawn into a rapture of love by God to union with God and wherein the soul's faculties, to a greater or lesser degree, are suspended and within which a deepened love for God and neighbor and supernatural insights are produced (author's definition).

Examen/examination of conscience: Reflection in God's presence on the state of one's soul that has some reference to a specific adopted standard of conduct (e.g., a rule of life or commitments) (author's adaptation).

Examen—particular: Regular prayerful examination of one's conscience by concentrating on some one particular moral failing to be overcome or virtue to be exercised. Its focus is on such external manifestations of the fault or virtue as can be remembered for periodic inventory. The subjects for particular examen are changed weekly, monthly, or otherwise in order to ensure maximum attention. They are also commonly associated with some brief invocation for divine assistance, as occasions arise for avoiding a sin or acting on a virtue. And after some time, another cycle may be started of the same defects that this person has to conquer or good habits he or she needs to develop.

Faculties: Powers of the mind, such as reason, memory, intellect, awareness, and so forth (author's definition).

Formation: The act or process of developing someone in all realms of human experience, but in particular those that help the human person come to better know and love God and serve others. Although human guides may assist this process, we are formed by God, as illustrated through the imagery of the potter (God) and the clay (soul) (author's definition).

Grace: In biblical language the condescension or benevolence (Greek *charis*) shown by God toward the human race; it is also the unmerited gift proceeding from this benevolent disposition. Grace, therefore, is a totally gratuitous gift on which man has absolutely no claim. Where on occasion the Scriptures speak of grace as pleasing charm or thanks for favors received, this is a derived and not primary use of the term.

As the Church has come to explain the meaning of grace, it refers to something more than the gifts of nature, such as creation or the blessings of bodily health. Grace is the supernatural gift that

God, of His free benevolence, bestows on rational creatures for their eternal salvation. The gifts of grace are essentially supernatural. They surpass the being, powers, and claims of created nature, namely, sanctifying grace, the infused virtues, the gifts of the Holy Spirit, and actual grace. They are the indispensable means necessary to reach the beatific vision. In a secondary sense, grace also includes such blessings as the miraculous gifts of prophecy or healing, or the preternatural gifts of freedom from concupiscence.

The essence of grace, properly so called, is its gratuity, since no creature has a right to the beatific vision, and its finality or purpose is to lead one to eternal life.

Imperfections: Deficiencies of character that, although not as serious as mortal or venial sins, are nonetheless obstacles to attaining Christian perfection and union with God. It is important to note that the intentional omission of an obligatory good act is sinful (e.g., missing Mass on Sunday without sufficient reason). However, the failure to do a good act that is *not* obligatory (e.g., not going to daily Mass), whether through human frailty or the difficulty of judging its obligation, is considered a moral imperfection. While imperfections reflect deficiencies in our character and are obstacles to Christian perfection, they are not sins and therefore are insufficient matter for absolution. However, they may be confessed in order to settle one's conscience and to grow in the spiritual life. The scrupulous would constitute an exception and should follow the guidance of their confessor or spiritual director in such matters (author's definition).

Infused prayer: See "Prayer—contemplation—infused."

Locution: A supernatural communication to the ear, imagination, or directly to the intellect. The locution is supernatural in the manner of communication, that is, beyond the ordinary laws of nature. Spurious locutions may come from the evil spirit and can be recognized by their lack of coherence or clarity, the disquiet they cause in the one who receives them, and the evil effects they produce in those who listen to them.

Magisterium: The Church's teaching authority, vested in the bishops, as successors of the apostles, under the Roman Pontiff, as successor of St. Peter. Also vested in the pope, as Vicar of Christ and visible head of the Catholic Church.

Movement: An ecclesial organization with canonical recognition that provides defined paths to living out baptismal commitments, discipleship, and related sanctity through a specific spiritual lens called a "charism" that is expressed by distinctive practices of life and ways of prayer (author's definition).

Mysticism: The supernatural state of soul in which God is known in a way that no human effort or exertion could ever succeed in producing. There is an immediate, personal experience of God that is truly extraordinary, not only in intensity and degree, but in kind. It is always the result of a special, totally unmerited grace of God. Christian mysticism differs essentially from the non-Christian mysticism of the Oriental world. It always recognizes that the reality to which it penetrates simply transcends the soul and the cosmos; there is no confusion between *I* and *thou*, but always a profound humility before the infinite Majesty of God. And in Christian mysticism all union between the soul and God is a moral union of love, in doing His will even at great sacrifice to self; there is no hint of losing one's being in God or absorption of one's personality into the divine.

Particular examen: See "Examen—particular."

Penance: The virtue or disposition of heart by which one repents of one's own sins and is converted to God. Also, the punishment by which one atones for sins committed, either by oneself or by others. And finally, the Sacrament of Penance, where confessed sins committed after Baptism are absolved by a priest in the name of God.

Perfection: The state in which nothing is lacking that, according to its nature, someone or something should possess. That which in itself has all possible excellence and excludes all deficiencies is absolutely perfect. Only God is absolutely perfect. That which has a finite nature and possesses all the advantages corresponding to its nature is relatively perfect. The Church teaches that God is infinite in every perfection. Creatures are as perfect as they are like God, and moral perfection consists in becoming like Christ, who is infinite God in human form (author's adaptation).

Piety: The religious sensibility of a person that reflects an attitude of reverence, respect, and devotion toward God and the things of God (author's definition).

Prayer—affective: Often the result of discursive meditation (see below), affective prayer occurs when the heart and mind are engaged, with and beyond the intellect, with the object of the meditation (author's definition).

Prayer—contemplation—infused: An infused supernatural gift that originates completely outside of our will or ability in God, by which a person becomes freely absorbed in God producing a real awareness, desire, and love for Him. This often gentle or delightful or even nonsensory encounter can yield special insights into things of the spirit and results in a deeper and tangible desire to love God and neighbor in thought, word, and deed. It is important to note that infused contemplation is a state that can be prepared for, but cannot in any way be produced, by the will or desire of a person through methods or ascetical practices (author's definition).

Prayer — meditation: Reflective prayer. It is that form of mental prayer in which the mind, in God's presence, thinks about God and divine things. While the affections may also be active, the stress in meditation is on the role of the intellect. Hence, this is also called discursive mental prayer. The objects of meditation are mainly three: mysteries of faith; a person's better knowledge of what God wants him or her to do; and the divine will, to know how God wants to be served by the one who is meditating.

Prayer — mental prayer: Filling the heart and mind with God. The form of prayer in which the sentiments expressed are one's own and not those of another person, and the expression of these sentiments is mainly, if not entirely, interior and not externalized (that is, not vocalized). Mental prayer is accomplished by internal acts of the mind and affections that are a loving and discursive (reflective) consideration of religious truths or some mystery of faith. In mental prayer, the three powers of the soul are engaged: the memory, which offers the mind material for meditation; the intellect, which ponders or directly perceives the meaning of some religious truth and its implications for practice; and the will, which freely expresses its sentiments of faith, trust, and love and (as needed) makes good resolutions based on what the memory and intellect have made known to the will (adapted from Fr. Hardon by the author).

Prayer — prayer of simplicity: Meditation replaced by a purer, more intimate prayer consisting in a simple regard for or loving thought of God, or of one of His attributes, or of some mystery of the Christian Faith. The soul peacefully attends to the operations of the Spirit with sentiments of love without requiring the use of mental effort (adapted from Fr. Hardon by the author).

Prayer — vocal: Any form of prayer expressed audibly using pre-written formulas (e.g., the Rosary and the Liturgy of the Hours).

Predominant fault: The defect in us that tends to prevail over the others, and thereby over our manner of feeling, judging, sympathizing, willing, and acting. It is a defect that has in each of us an intimate relation to our individual temperament.[65]

Purgation: The experience of being purged or pruned by God to rid of things that hinder our spiritual progress to union with God (author's definition).

Purification — active: This purification comes about as a result of the efforts of the soul (aided by the Holy Spirit) who seeks to purify itself from sins, vices, imperfections, and anything that would keep it from attaining to holiness, union with God, and living a life that honors God and neighbor (author's definition).

Purification — passive: This purification shares the same end as active purification whose means are solely of God and from God. This purification is the preparation for the exceptional graces of the supernatural life (author's definition).

Recollection: Concentration of soul on the presence of God usually in the context of the focus of heart and mind in mental prayer.

---

[65] See Fr. Reginald Garrigou-Lagrange, *The Three Ages of the Interior Life*, part 2, chap. 22.

Renunciation: To give up something to which a person has a claim. Some renunciations are necessary by divine law; others are permitted and encouraged according to divine counsel. Everyone must renounce sin and those creatures that are proximate occasions to sin. In this category belongs the renunciation of Satan at Baptism, either by the person being baptized or by the sponsor. Renunciations of counsel pertain to the exercise of such natural rights as material possessions, marriage, and legitimate autonomy or self-determination, sacrificed for love of God by those who vow themselves to poverty, chastity, and obedience.

Reparation: The act or fact of making amends. It implies an attempt to restore things to their normal or sound conditions, as they were before something wrong was done. It applies mainly to recompense for the losses sustained or the harm caused by some morally bad action. With respect to God, it means making up with greater love for the failure in love through sin; it means restoring what was unjustly taken and compensating with generosity for the selfishness that caused the jury.

Root sin: See "Predominant fault."

Rule of life: A specific and usually documented plan for living in accord with one's state in life and baptismal commitments that includes principals, guidelines, and commitments that will guide each person to achieve sanctity and, in practical and concrete ways, love God and love their neighbor. A principle or regular mode of action, prescribed by one in authority, for the well-being of those who are members of a society. It is in this sense that the organized methods of living the evangelical counsels are called rules, as the Rule of St. Augustine or St. Benedict. A rule may also be a customary standard that is not necessarily prescribed by authority, but voluntarily undertaken in order to regulate one's conduct for more effective moral living or more effective service of others (author's definition).

Scrupulosity: The habit of imagining sin where none exists, or grave sin where the matter is venial. To overcome scrupulosity, a person needs to be properly instructed in order to form a right conscience, and in extreme cases the only remedy is absolute obedience (for a time) to a prudent confessor.

Self-annihilation: Heroic renunciation and self-giving. See "Renunciation."

Self-denial: The act or practice of giving up some legitimate satisfaction for the sake of some higher motive.

Self-knowledge: Personal awareness of both the dignity of the human soul and its exalted destiny, as well as knowledge of the wounds and darkness that original and personal sin have inflicted on it. This awareness is not one that is isolated to the natural order, but one that frames self-understanding in the context of God's presence and God's law (author's definition).

Sensible consolation: Those consolations that are experienced in the sensory faculties — that is, they can be recognized as "feelings" (author's definition).

Sin — mortal: An actual sin that destroys sanctifying grace and causes the supernatural death of the soul. Mortal sin is a turning away from God because of a seriously inordinate adherence to created things that causes grave injury to a person's rational nature and to the social order and deprives the sinner of a right to Heaven. The terms "mortal," "deadly," "grave," and "serious"

applied to sin are synonyms, each with a slightly different impli-
cation. "Mortal" and "deadly" focus on the effects in the sinner,
namely, deprivation of the state of friendship with God; "grave"
and "serious" refer to the importance of the matter in which a
person offends God. But the Church never distinguishes among
these terms as though they represented different kinds of sins.
There is only one recognized correlative to mortal sin, and that
is venial sin, which offends against God but does not cause the
loss of one's state of grace. The three conditions necessary for a
sin to be mortal are grave matter, full knowledge, and full consent
(the last line adapted by the author from the *Catechism of the
Catholic Church*, no. 1857).

Sin — occasion of: Any person, place, or thing that of its nature
or because of human frailty can lead one to do wrong, thereby
committing sin. If the danger is certain and probable, the occasion is proximate; if the danger is slight, the occasion becomes
remote. It is voluntary if it can easily be avoided. There is no
obligation to avoid a remote occasion unless there is probable
danger of its becoming proximate. There is a positive obligation
to avoid a voluntary proximate occasion of sin even though the
occasion of evildoing is due only to human weakness.

Sin — venial: An offense against God which does not deprive
the sinner of sanctifying grace. It is called venial (from *venia*
pardon) because the soul still has the vital principle that allows
a cure from within, similar to the healing of a sick or diseased
body whose source of animation (the soul) is still present to
restore the ailing bodily function to health. Deliberate venial
sin is a disease that slackens the spiritual powers, lowers one's
resistance to evil, and causes one to deviate from the path
that leads to heavenly glory. Variously called "daily sins" or

"light sins" or "lesser sins," they are committed under a variety of conditions: when a person transgresses with full or partial knowledge and consent to a divine law that does not oblige seriously; when one violates a law that obliges gravely, but either one's knowledge or consent is not complete; or when one disobeys what is an objectively grave precept but, due to invincible ignorance, a person thinks the obligation is not serious. The essence of venial sin consists in a certain disorder but does not imply complete aversion from humanity's final destiny. It is an illness of the soul rather than its supernatural death. When people commit a venial sin, they do not decisively set themselves on turning away from God, but from over-fondness for some created good fall short of God. They are like persons who loiter without leaving the way.

Spiritual exercises or disciplines: Any set program of religious duties, notably the prayers, meditations, and spiritual reading required of persons following a distinctive rule of life. Also, the period of silence and prayerful reflection practiced annually (or more often) in a retreat. Particularly the *Spiritual Exercises* by St. Ignatius Loyola, drawn up as a method of arriving at the amendment of one's life and resolving on a determined way of holiness. The *Exercises* of St. Ignatius were first composed by him in a cave at Manresa, in Spain, after his conversion. They have been recommended by successive popes as a most effective program of spiritual renewal for priests, religious, and the laity. Their underlying principle is their opening statement that "man was created to praise, reverence and serve our Creator and Lord, and by this means to save his soul." Given this basic purpose of human existence, the believer is told how to reach his or her destiny by overcoming sinful tendencies and imitating Christ in carrying the Cross on earth in order to be glorified with Christ in the life to come.

Temperament: The distinctive emotional, mental, and affective qualities of each individual. A classic position holds that there are four basic temperaments: phlegmatic, or not easily aroused; choleric, or having a low threshold for anger; sanguine, or optimistic and free from anxiety; and melancholic, or given to introspection and pessimism about the future. No single person, it is agreed, has only one temperament, although one or the other trait will predominate.

Virtue: A good habit that enables a person to act according to right reason enlightened by faith. Also called an operative good habit, it makes its possessor a good person and his or her actions also good.

Vision: Supernatural perception of some object that is not visible naturally. A vision is a revelation only when the object seen also discloses some hidden truth or mystery.

About the Author

Dan Burke is the founder and president of the Avila Institute for Spiritual Formation, which offers graduate and personal enrichment studies in spiritual theology to priests, deacons, religious, and laity in more than ninety countries and prepares men for seminary in thirty-six dioceses.

Dan is the author or editor of more than fifteen books on authentic Catholic spirituality and with his wife, Stephanie, hosts the *Divine Intimacy Radio* show, which is broadcast weekly on EWTN Radio. Past episodes, along with thousands of articles on the interior life, can be found at SpiritualDirection.com.

In his deep commitment to the advancement of faithful Catholic spirituality, he is also the founder of Apostoli Viae, a worldwide, private association of the faithful dedicated to living and advancing the contemplative life.

Most importantly, Dan is a blessed husband, father of four, and grandfather of one—and is grateful to be Catholic.

A special thanks to our *Devil in the Castle* launch team, who read this book before publication and helped us with promotion. Thank you for your time and enthusiasm.

Friends of Avila, Adam and Leah Drexler, Alexander Lewis, Ally J. Brown, Amanda Robben, Amy and Danny Ryan, Amy E. Shaffer, Andrea Ulrich, Andy & Barbara Parrish, Angel de la Garza, Angela Oprendek, Ann Virnig, Anne O'Connell, Anonymous, Avis , Baby Reuter, Barbara Sanders, Barbara Zupcsan, Becky Malmquist, Beth Crawford, Biz Blee, Brad and Geraldine Rupp, Brenda L. Bath Conyers, Brian and Kelly Schroepfer, Brooke Pittner, Candace MacMillan, Carmen Braaten, Carmen Milagros O. Reyes, Carol Joyce, Carol Slade, Carolyn Hunter Denny, Cathleen Ludlow, Cathy Trowbridge, Cheri Moyce Everett, Chris and Elyse Berninger, Chris Lahn, Christa Lopiccolo, Christine Arata, Christine Stephens, Cindy Prochazka, Claire Dwyer, Colleen Morrison, Cris and Jeff Davis, Damian Borda, Daniel John Galloway, David and Heather Chapman, Dawn Powell, Debbie Aguiar, Deborah Honemann, Denise D. Andrin, Diana von Glahn, Diane Roe, DiFuccia Family, Dom & Maggie Cingoranelli, Dr. Joseph Hollcraft, Dr. Paul Fox, Dr. Susanne Moskalski, Ed and Karen Lieber, Edgard L. Riba, Elaine Knight, Elizabeth Mathew, Eric & Lisa Hoyer, Father Brent Maher, Fr. Jim Boland, Fr. Matthew MacDonald, Fr. Thomas and Janet Wray, Frank and Helene Biller, Geetha Fernandes, Gerald & Nadia Rhodes, Gina Witt, Glenn and Cammi Dickinson, Gloria L Huck, Greg & Joyce Forchuk, Greg and Colleen Lang, Gregory Delozier, Heather Voccola, Holy Souls in Purgatory, James Jackson, Jamie Gidley, Jan C. Schnack, Janet Zazulak, Jennifer Corgan, Jérôme Rajoely, Jerry & Christine Locke, Jerry & Deborah Cable, Jerry Tiarsmith, Jim and Kathy Bohn, Joan and Bill Stewart, Joené, John & Kathy Springer, John and Karen Whelan, John Hoehn, John Nolan Hoyer, Jordan Burke, Josh Meeker, Josie Showmaker , Judith

McGuinn, Judy Silhan, Juliana Iarossi, Julie and Tim Foley, Julie Habiger, Karen Davidian, Karen Marie Stanford Bonvecchio, Kathi Carey, Kathleen Beckman, Kathleen Forck, Kathleen Johnson, Kim Capman, Kimberly Pérez, Kimberly Rayer, Kris and Barbata Shekitka, Kristin Priola, Kristina Bellock Gillespie, Kristina Olson, Lady Carmel F. Cole, Laura Ashley Maurizzi, Laura Daniel, Lauren Whittaker, Laurie Manhardt, Leah Ann Phillips, Lesia Petrizio, Linda Tan, Lisa A. Nicholas, Ph. D., Lisa Marie Bald, Lois Ann Mader, Lonnie Applegate, Luke & Jacqueline Novak, Lynette Wijnveldt, Maggie Herd, Marc and Trish Hurtgen, Marcela Montemayor, Margaret Monzani, Marian Mazzone, Mario Uribe III, Mark and Teresa Drotts, Mark DeLaurentis, Mary Ellen Jackson, Mary Ellen Roemer, Mary Lawrence, Mary Wynne, Matt & Sonia Sonnier, Meg and Max Koss, Melissa Holt, Michael Forck, Michael Mulski, Michelle Meza, Mr. Anderson Lopez, Mrs. Darlene Lewinski, Mrs. Dora Donovan, Mrs. Carmen L. Fletcher, Mrs. Crystal Gordon, Mrs. Patricia Blake, Mrs. Suzi Dutro, Mrs. William Garland, Nalina & Bernard Chinnasami, Norma, Oren Donald & Michelle Long, Pamela J. Schaefer, Patrick Booth, Paul and Christina Semmens, Paul Mustoe, Peggy Angstadt, Peggy Hobby, Peggy Hool, Pequeño Family, Randy and Candace MacMillan, Raymond Aguiar, Rick and Joanne Harris, Rita K Levine, Robert & Diane Schwind, Robert and Melinda Sass, Robert G. Conway, Jr., MDiv, JD, Robin Sellers, Sandra Buffalano, Sarah Yurgelaitis, Scott H. Heekin-Canedy, Shirley Folwarski OCDS, Stephen A Andrin, Susan Gwyer, Susan Heroux, Susan Meyers Wenzel, Susan Moore, Susan Mulski, Suzanne C. Hurtig, Suzi Dutro, Tamara Jones Andersson, Teresa Margolis, The Antonovich Family, The Baier Family, The Bardin Family, The Burditt Family, The Cardali Family, The Cardillo Family, The Casali Family, The Castle Family, The De Witt Family, The Dupuis Family, The Dutton Family, The Forchuk Family, The Fossier Family, The George Family, The Gioiello Family, The Hahn Family, The Hennessy Family, The Jordan Family, The Leal

Family, The Leon Family, The McKinniss Family, The Meister Family, The Muller Family, The Nite Family, The Pizzuto Family, The Rich Family, The Rogge Family, The Scott Family, The Sillin Family, The Tandarich Family, The Taylor Family, The Tuman Family, The V. and A. Fritz family, The Walter Family, The Webb Family, The Wurster Family, The Zaar Family, Theresa Brown, Tim and Mary Becker, Tina Marie Tocco, Tish Grijalva, Tom Hornacek, Wilma Drummer, Young Souls

Sophia Institute

Sophia Institute is a nonprofit institution that seeks to nurture the spiritual, moral, and cultural life of souls and to spread the gospel of Christ in conformity with the authentic teachings of the Roman Catholic Church.

Sophia Institute Press fulfills this mission by offering translations, reprints, and new publications that afford readers a rich source of the enduring wisdom of mankind.

Sophia Institute also operates the popular online resource CatholicExchange.com. *Catholic Exchange* provides world news from a Catholic perspective as well as daily devotionals and articles that will help readers to grow in holiness and live a life consistent with the teachings of the Church.

In 2013, Sophia Institute launched Sophia Institute for Teachers to renew and rebuild Catholic culture through service to Catholic education. With the goal of nurturing the spiritual, moral, and cultural life of souls, and an abiding respect for the role and work of teachers, we strive to provide materials and programs that are at once enlightening to the mind and ennobling to the heart; faithful and complete, as well as useful and practical.

Sophia Institute gratefully recognizes the Solidarity Association for preserving and encouraging the growth of our apostolate over the course of many years. Without their generous and timely support, this book would not be in your hands.

www.SophiaInstitute.com
www.CatholicExchange.com
www.SophiaInstituteforTeachers.org

Sophia Institute Press® is a registered trademark of Sophia Institute.
Sophia Institute is a tax-exempt institution as defined by the
Internal Revenue Code, Section 501(c)(3). Tax ID 22-2548708.